Why Do ENGLISH LANGUAGE LEARNERS

Struggle With **Reading?**

D0731192

We wish to dedicate this book to the students we had the privilege of teaching who were English language learners and labeled as having learning disabilities: Elvia, Jorge, Francisco, Azucena, Veronica, Richard, and Yulexis—to name only a few. Some of these students had learning disabilities, but many did not. It was their challenges and successes, their frustrations and their joys, that planted the seeds for this book so many years ago.

Why Do ENGLISH LANGUAGE LEARNERS
Struggle With **Reading?**

Distinguishing Language Acquisition
From Learning Disabilities

Janette K. Klingner

John J. Hoover

Leonard M. Baca

Editors

CORWIN PRESS
A SAGE Company
Thousand Oaks, CA 91320

For information:

Corwin Press
A SAGE Company
2455 Teller Road
Thousand Oaks, California 91320
www.corwinpress.com

SAGE India Pvt. Ltd.
B 1/I 1 Mohan Cooperative
   Industrial Area
Mathura Road, New Delhi 110 044
India

SAGE Ltd.
1 Oliver's Yard
55 City Road
London EC1Y 1SP
United Kingdom

SAGE Asia-Pacific Pte. Ltd.
33 Pekin Street #02–01
Far East Square
Singapore 048763

Printed in the United States of America.

Library of Congress Cataloging-in-Publication Data

Klingner, Janette K. Why do English language learners struggle with reading?: distinguishing language acquisition from learning disabilities/Janette K. Klingner, John J. Hoover, and Leonard M. Baca.
    p. cm.
Includes bibliographical references and index.
ISBN 978-1-4129-4146-4 (cloth)
ISBN 978-1-4129-4147-1 (pbk.)
    1. Reading disability—United States. 2. Learning disabilities—United States.
3. Second language acquisition. 4. English language—Study and teaching—United States. I. Hoover, John J. II. Baca, Leonard M. III. Title.

LB1050.5.K543 2008
372.43--dc22   2008004895

This book is printed on acid-free paper.

         10 11 12 10 9 8 7 6 5 4 3

Acquisitions Editor:	David Chao
Editorial Assistant:	Mary Dang
Production Editor:	Eric Garner
Copy Editor:	Gretchen Treadwell
Typesetter:	C&M Digitals (P) Ltd.
Proofreader:	Theresa Kay
Indexer:	Sheila Bodell
Cover Designer:	Karine Hovsepian

Contents

Preface

We have devoted our careers to trying to improve educational opportunities and outcomes for culturally and linguistically diverse students, especially English language learners. In our several years of work as teachers and as professors preparing teachers, we have noticed that one of the most challenging aspects of working with English language learners is determining why they might be underachieving. In some cases, it is that they are not being taught in environments conducive to learning or with instructional practices that are appropriate for meeting their needs. Perhaps they are struggling with English language acquisition. Or, they might truly have learning disabilities. In fact, all of the above might be contributing to English language learners' slow progress.

The first step in providing students with support that is well-matched to their needs is determining the reasons for their difficulties. Thus, the purpose of this book is to help practitioners distinguish between learning disabilities and other possible explanations for children's struggles in school. We provide readers with a wealth of information about different aspects of this important educational challenge. It is our hope that as teachers and other support personnel read through the different chapters of this book, they will reflect on their own practices, discuss the content of the book with their colleagues, and apply what they are learning with their students. We envision that the reader will become more confident and competent in determining why English language learners might be struggling.

Acknowledgments

This book is sponsored by the National Center for Culturally Responsive Educational Systems (NCCRESt). There are many individuals along the way who helped with its construction whose contributions we would like to acknowledge. First, we wish to thank Dr. Grace Zamora Durán. It was her expert guidance as the project officer for NCCRESt that provided the impetus for this work. Secondly, we would like to acknowledge the invaluable assistance of Dr. Alfredo Artiles, coprincipal investigator for NCCRESt, whose conceptual contributions helped to frame our approach to the book. Next, we would like to thank the authors who contributed to different book chapters and helped make the book a reality: Estella Almanza de Schonewise, Carmen de Onis, Diana Geisler, Laura Méndez Barletta, Todd Fletcher, and Michael J. Orosco. Finally, we would like to show our appreciation for the researchers who coauthored papers presented at NCCRESt's National Research Conference, "English Language Learners Struggling to Learn: Emergent Research on Linguistic Differences and Learning Disabilities," November 18–19, 2004: Jamal Abedi, Alfredo Artiles, Manuel Barrera, Judith Bernhard, Paul Cirino, Jim Cummins, Kathy Escamilla, Richard Figueroa, Todd Fletcher, Margaret Gallego, Eugene Garcia, Michael Gerber, Diane Haager, Beth Harry, Nonie Lesaux, Sylvia Linan-Thompson, Jeff MacSwan, Laura Méndez Barletta, Patricia Newsome, Alba Ortiz, Kathryn Prater, Elba Reyes, Phyllis Robertson, Robert Rueda, Richard Ruiz, Guillermo Solano Flores, Sharon Vaughn, Cheryl Wilkinson, Michelle Windmueller, and Grace Zamora-Durán. Their research served as the foundation for the chapters in this book.

Corwin Press would also like to thank the following for their professional contributions to the book:

Juliana Arazi
ESL teacher
Urbana School District 116
Urbana, IL

About the Editors

Janette K. Klingner was a bilingual special education teacher for ten years before earning a PhD in Reading and Learning Disabilities from the University of Miami. Recent coauthored or coedited books include *Teaching Reading Comprehension to Students With Learning Difficulties* (Guilford, 2007), *Methods for Teaching Culturally and Linguistically Diverse Exceptional Learners* (Merrill/Prentice Hall, 2008), *Case Studies in the Social Construction of Disability: Minority Students in Special Education* (Teachers College Press, 2007), *Evidence-Based Practices for Response to Intervention* (Brookes, 2007), and *Why Are So Many Minority Students in Special Education? Understanding Race and Disability in Schools* (Teachers College Press, 2006).

John J. Hoover is a former K–12 special education teacher for students with learning disabilities and emotional/behavior disorders in several states in the Midwest, West, and Southwest. He earned a BA in Elementary and Special Education (Mental Retardation), an MA in Learning Disabilities and Emotional Disorders with an emphasis in Reading, and a PhD in Curriculum specializing in Special Education. Publications include his forthcoming book—*Differentiating Learning Differences From Learning and Behavioral Disabilities: Teaching Diverse Learners Through Multi-Tiered Response to Intervention* (Allyn & Bacon) and recent books coauthored/coedited—*Methods for Teaching Culturally and Linguistically Diverse Exceptional Learners* (Pearson Merrill, 2008); *Curriculum Adaptations for Students With Learning and Behavior Problems: Differentiating Instruction to Meet Diverse Needs* (Pro-Ed, 2005); and *Teaching Study Skills to Students With Learning Problems* (Pro-Ed, 2007). His forthcoming tests include the *Early Literacy Measure* (Pro-Ed) and the *Behavior Skills Rating System* (Pro-Ed).

 **Leonard M. Baca** has an EdD from the University of Northern Colorado. He has been a professor of Education at the University of Colorado at Boulder since 1973. He has taught courses in bilingual and bilingual special education and served as the program chair. Professor Baca is founder and Director of the BUENO Center for Multicultural Education. He is the author of *The Bilingual Special Education Interface* (Merrill Prentice Hall, 2004) and several other articles dealing with English language learners with disabilities.

Introduction

Many English language learners (ELLs) in our schools seem to struggle with reading. Why? What can educators do? *Why Do English Language Learners Struggle With Reading?: Distinguishing Language Acquisition From Learning Disabilities* provides educators with information designed to help determine whether their ELLs are struggling with reading because they may have learning disabilities (LD) or for some other reason associated with second language acquisition. Simultaneously, we attempt to clarify many of the misconceptions surrounding ELL instruction and assessment.

The unprecedented growth of the ELL population, concerns about the number of inappropriate referrals of ELLs to special education, the challenges associated with distinguishing between reading difficulties related to second language acquisition and problems caused by LD, along with the alarming scarcity of research on these and related issues, strongly suggest the importance of and need for this practical book. With increased momentum nationwide to provide evidence-based instruction to all students, it is essential to revisit some of the more pressing issues that have challenged educators of ELLs who struggle with learning, particularly in reading.

Our goal is to provide solutions to the challenges educators face as they work to address the recurring needs of ELLs. In each chapter, we describe a different aspect of distinguishing between language acquisition and LD. Chapters include numerous guides, checklists, figures, and tables for easy reference and use by practitioners. It is our hope that they will facilitate data-gathering and decision making efforts to provide the most appropriate education to ELLs, while simultaneously reducing their inappropriate referral and placement into special education.[1]

---

1. This book is based in part on a series of research papers presented at a 2004 conference on English language learners. This conference was held in Tempe, Arizona, and was cosponsored by the National Center for Culturally Responsive Educational Systems (NCCRESt) and Arizona State University, with support from the National Association for Bilingual Education (NABE) and the Council for Exceptional Children (CEC). This book is sponsored by NCCRESt.

U.S. schools are currently undergoing a transformation. The reauthorized Individuals with Disabilities Education Improvement Act (IDEA; 2004) included momentous changes intended to significantly alter the ways schools support student learning and identify students as having LD. No longer is a discrepancy between intelligence and achievement needed as part of the special education identification process. Instead, educators are encouraged to determine the extent to which students respond to research-based interventions. As a result, schools are scrambling to implement multi-tiered response to intervention (RTI) models. Although RTI models are new to most practitioners and require a paradigm shift in how we think about helping students, some of the same practices and principles previously used as part of the special education process are still mandated by current law (i.e., IDEA, 2004). It is against this backdrop that we have written this book. We describe RTI models for diverse schools and clarify which practices and procedures are similar to and different from previous approaches.

In Chapter 1, we provide background information intended to set the stage for future chapters. We detail demographic information about the diverse ELL population in the United States and explain what we know about the disproportionate representation of ELLs in special education. Then we present a brief description of LD, finishing the chapter with an overview of what we know from research about distinguishing between LD and language acquisition among ELLs.

In Chapter 2, we focus on the language acquisition process. We pay particular attention to common misconceptions about second language acquisition that can be confusing for educators and contribute to misperceptions about language delay or LD. For each of eight misconceptions, we explain what we know from research about the realities of that aspect of the language acquisition process among ELLs in U.S. schools.

In Chapter 3, we describe RTI models for ELLs. First we provide an overview of RTI, and then we discuss assumptions underlying RTI that can be problematic when applied in schools with high percentages of ELLs. This chapter also illustrates challenges schools may face as they attempt to implement RTI for the first time. For each difficulty, we discuss possible solutions.

In Chapter 4, we tackle the very real challenges classroom teachers face while teaching reading to their ELLs. It is classroom teachers who most often first notice that a child is not progressing, and classroom teachers who may first suspect that a child might have LD. We explain what we know from research about how literacy instruction differs for ELLs, and focus on helping classroom teachers distinguish between second language acquisition and LD among ELLs by explaining some of the struggles ELLs face when learning to read in English.

In Chapter 5, we portray data-driven decision making in a multi-tiered model. We discuss factors teachers should consider when their ELLs first show signs of struggling, and provide a chart in which we compare and contrast characteristics of LD and language acquisition. In addition, we point out ways that RTI is similar to and different from previous pre-referral models, and offer practical guidelines regarding what kinds of data to consider when making decisions about students.

In Chapter 6, we outline issues to consider when assessing ELLs for possible special education placement. This chapter focuses on assessment as used for eligibility, identification, and diagnostic purposes. We discuss the validity of tests for assessing the performance of ELLs and point out the impact of regional and dialectal differences on test scores, providing specific examples with actual test items. In addition, the chapter includes an overall ecological model for assessment.

In Chapter 7, our conclusion, we focus on "putting the pieces together." Using the analogy of a puzzle, we note how each previous chapter adds to our understanding of ELLs who struggle with reading and how to determine whether they may have LD or are simply manifesting expected signs of the language acquisition process. At the end of our conclusion, we provide a wrap-up of the topics explored in this book and discuss possible future directions for practitioners.

We hope that practitioners at both elementary and secondary levels of education will find the practical ideas, suggestions, guides, and checklists valuable resources as they continue with their own professional growth to best meet the educational needs of English language learners with or without disabilities.

Distinguishing Between Language Acquisition and Learning Disabilities Among English Language Learners

Background Information

Michael J. Orosco, Estella Almanza de Schonewise,
Carmen de Onis, Janette K. Klingner,
and John J. Hoover

First, who are English language learners? English language learners (ELLs) are students who speak a language other than English as their first language and who are in the process of acquiring English as a second or additional language. They are not yet fully proficient in English. For this reason, we might refer to them as "emerging bilinguals." Some are immigrants; others were born in the United States. Their demographic characteristics vary widely. In this chapter, we begin with a comprehensive overview of the changing demographics associated with ELLs in today's schools, providing a summary by Garcia (2004) of ELL demographics as a backdrop to the discussions that follow in subsequent chapters regarding the linguistic and literacy development of ELLs. We then present a brief description of the phenomenon of disproportionate representation, next describe learning disabilities, and finish the chapter with an overview of what we know from research about distinguishing between learning disabilities and language acquisition among ELLs.

ELL DEMOGRAPHICS

Garcia (2004) characterized the presence of ELLs in this nation as "large-scale . . . with no signs of abating soon" (p. 13). Immigrants now comprise approximately 11 percent of the U.S. population, the highest percentage in 70 years (Garcia, 2001). According to the Center for Immigration Studies, the immigrant population in the United States tripled from 1970 to 2000, increasing from 9.6 to 28.4 million immigrants. "Immigration accounts for virtually all of the national increase in public school enrollment over the last two decades. In 2000, there were 8.6 million school-aged children from immigrant families in the United States" (Garcia, 2004, p. 10). Over 4 million students enrolled in public schools were not yet fully proficient in English in the 1999–2000 school year, or 9.3 percent of the total public school student enrollment (Kendler, 2002). Demographic figures show the ELL population has more than doubled over the past decade.

In addition, the 2000 U.S. Census reported that 46,951,595 individuals ages 5 or older spoke a language other than English at home. This was a 47 percent increase in numbers reported in the 1990 U.S. Census. "Expected" growth occurred in states with a historically large representation of diverse populations, such as California (103 percent), Arizona (75 percent), and Texas (51 percent). There was also "unexpected" growth in states such as Georgia (164 percent), North Carolina (150 percent), and Arkansas (103 percent). While students speak many different languages in public schools, Spanish remains the language most frequently spoken by individuals who speak a language other than English in the United States, representing 75 percent of children with emerging English proficiency (Baca & Cervantes, 2004; Garcia, 2004; Special Issues Analysis Center, 1995). See Table 1.1 for a list of the most commonly spoken languages other than English in U.S. schools.

Immigrant ELLs vary in the extent to which they attended schools in their home countries. Garcia (2004) pointed out that "recent immigrants with high levels of education are disproportionately from several nations in east and south Asia, while those with little schooling are largely from a number of Latin American countries" (p. 14). In the United States, Mexicans represent the largest immigrant group and one of the least educated, which is significant to U.S. schools because children from families with high levels

Table 1.1   Top Ten Languages Spoken By Linguistically Diverse Populations in the United States

Rank (estimate)	Language	English Language Learners (estimate)	% of English Language Learners (estimate)
1	Spanish	3,598,451	79.045%
2	Vietnamese	88,906	1.953%
3	Hmong	70,768	1.555%
4	Chinese, Cantonese	46,466	1.021%
5	Korean	43,969	0.966%
6	Haitian Creole	42,236	0.928%
7	Arabic	41,279	0.907%
8	Russian	37,157	0.816%
9	Tagalog	34,133	0.750%
10	Navajo	27,029	0.594%

of education tend to have higher academic achievement than those from families with little formal education (Garcia, 2004; Rumbaut, 1997).

Garcia (2004) also identified trends in the economic and environmental conditions in which English language learners live. "Of the 21.9 million children less than six years of age in 1998 . . . five million (25%) were living in poverty" (p. 1). Over 50 percent of non-White children were living in poverty; 72 percent lived in racially isolated neighborhoods. The poverty rate for immigrants is 50 percent higher than for those born in the United States, and immigrants comprise 22 percent of all persons living in poverty (Camarota, 2001). Moreover, statistics show that the 100 districts with the largest numbers of children living in poverty house over 40 percent more children per school building than the nation's average, indicating disparities in schooling experiences faced by many non-White students in this nation (National Center for Educational Statistics, 2000).

The increase in the English language learner population continues to stymie practitioners because ELLs tend to underachieve in comparison with their White middle-class counterparts on indicators of academic success. For example, according to the National Assessment of Educational Progress (NAEP; U.S. Department of Education, 2003), in 2003 only 15 percent of Hispanic students, 37 percent of Asian/Pacific Islander students, and 16 percent of American Indian/Alaska Native students in the fourth grade read at proficient or advanced proficient levels (McCardle, Mele-McCarthy, & Leos, 2005). In addition, in 2000, the U.S. Department of Education reported that the high school completion rate for the general population (18–24 years of age) was approximately 86 percent. Hispanics lagged behind in high school completion in comparison to other racial groups, at 64.1 percent; Blacks were 83.7 percent, Whites 91.8 percent, and Asians 94.6 percent.

Hodgkinson (2005), a leading educational demographer, projects that if we were to spread ELLs around the country and in every classroom, one out of every nine students would be a second language learner. Demographers project that by the year 2025, this number will increase to one in every four students. The challenge today is "educating to high standards students from diverse language, culture, and social class groups" (Garcia, 2004, p. 5). Because the number of ELLs continues to grow at a rapid rate, it is more important than ever for schools to address misconceptions about how best to meet their needs, including minimizing potential cultural and/or linguistic mismatches between teacher and students.

Teacher Shortages

Supplying enough teachers who are prepared to teach ELLs is a challenge. According to the American Association for Employment in Education, a lack of qualified teachers for ELLs continues to plague school districts nationwide. Schools in every region of the United States report a shortage of both bilingual and ESL teachers, with the most significant shortages occurring in those states that have not traditionally had large immigrant populations (Barron & Menken, 2002).

ELLs and their families look to teachers to meet their needs and help them to be successful in our nation's schools, assisting them in the attainment of the "American Dream" (Ladson-Billings, 2005). When there are significant differences between the student's culture and the school's culture, teachers can easily misread students' aptitudes, intent, or abilities because of variations in styles of language use and interactional patterns. Secondly, when such cultural differences exist, teachers may utilize styles of instruction and/or discipline that are at odds with community norms (Delpit, 1995, p. 167).

Added to a lack of cultural awareness, many teachers have received little or no training in English as a second language (ESL), English language acquisition, or bilingual/bicultural education (Menken & Antunez, 2001), leading to a teaching force that is inadequately prepared to face the growing challenge of educating culturally and linguistically diverse learners. According to a 1999 NCES Report, teachers were least likely to report being very prepared for (1) integrating educational technology into the grade or subject taught, (2) addressing the needs of limited English proficient or culturally diverse students, and (3) addressing the needs of students with disabilities. Since teachers have the main responsibility and play an integral role in the education of ELLs, their preparation is crucial to student success.

Culturally and linguistically diverse teachers can have a positive effect on the increasingly diverse student population (Foster, 1993; Merino & Quintanar, 1989). However, while the number of ELLs is dramatically increasing, the number of culturally and linguistically diverse teachers is decreasing. The dwindling minority teaching force, combined with the lack of qualified personnel to meet the needs of the diverse population in our nation's schools, has resulted in a "mismatch" between the teaching force and diverse student populations. For this reason, it is especially important to provide resources to practicing teachers so that they can enhance their knowledge about teaching ELLs.

ELLS AND DISPROPORTIONATE REPRESENTATION

Disproportionate representation refers to "unequal proportions of culturally diverse students in special education programs" (Artiles & Trent, 2000, p. 514), and is often assessed by calculating a group's representation in a specific special education category in comparison with their proportion of the total school-aged population, or in reference to the representation of a comparison group, most often White students. There is no one agreed upon best way of determining disproportionate representation, and several procedures and formulas have been proposed and used throughout the history of this problem.[1] Whichever index we use, the disability categories in which we are mostly to see disproportionate representation are mental retardation, emotional/behavioral disorders, and LD. The most common ethnic groups involved in overrepresentation include African American, Chicano/Latino, American Indian, and a few subgroups of Asian American students (see Artiles & Trent, 2000; Donovan & Cross, 2002).

---

1. The *risk index*, or RI, is calculated by dividing the number of students in a given racial or ethnic category served in a given disability category by the total enrollment for that group in the school population. Thus, a risk index of six for African American students in a given category means that 6 percent of all African Americans were given that label. The *composition index* is calculated by dividing the number of students of a given racial or ethnic group enrolled in a particular disability category by the total number of students (summed across all groups) enrolled in that same disability category. The sum of composition indices for all the groups will total 100 percent. This index does not control for the baseline enrollment of a given group. Finally, the *odds ratio* divides the risk index of one group by the risk index of another (most often White) for comparative purposes. Odds ratios greater than 1.0 indicate greater risk of identification.

Concerns about disproportionate representation focus on the "judgmental" categories of special education, or, in other words, those disabilities usually identified by school personnel rather than a medical professional after the child has started school (Klingner et al., 2005). The school personnel making placement decisions typically exercise wide latitude in deciding who qualifies for special education through a process that is quite subjective (Gottlieb, Alter, Gottlieb, & Wishner, 1994; Harry & Klingner, 2006). Notably, overrepresentation does not exist in low-incidence disability categories (such as visual, auditory, or orthopedic impairment; Donovan & Cross, 2002).

When we examine changes in special education identification over the years, one of the most striking findings is the "epidemic" increase in the risk of children of all racial/ethnic groups except Asian/Pacific Islanders for the LD category (Donovan & Cross, 2002, p. 47). Looking at current national averages, Hispanic/Latino students are only slightly overrepresented in programs for students with LD (Klingner et al., 2005). However, placement rates vary widely across states and districts. In some schools, Latino students are actually underrepresented in LD programs based on what would be expected given their percentage in the overall school population. In other schools, they are overrepresented. Artiles, Rueda, Salazar, and Higareda (2005) examined placement patterns in special education programs in 11 urban districts in California with high proportions of ELLs and high poverty levels. They found that ELLs were not overrepresented in LD in the primary grades, but were overrepresented in grades five and higher. Secondary level ELLs were almost twice as likely to be placed in special education than their peers. Furthermore, ELLs in English Immersion programs, where there was no primary language support, were almost three times more likely to be identified for special education than ELL students in bilingual classrooms. This work suggests that specific patterns become obscured when data are aggregated above district levels (Rueda & Windmueller, 2006). It also suggests the need to broaden examinations of disproportionate representation to include language proficiency in addition to ethnicity.

There are numerous possible reasons for disproportionate representation (Harry & Klingner, 2006). Because ELLs tend to underachieve in comparison with their mainstream counterparts, this puts pressure on practitioners to find ways to give the ELL student extra assistance to help close the achievement gap. Practitioners may perceive that special education is the only viable option for providing this support and refer the child to special education, or mistakenly assume that the student's struggles are due to LD rather than a normal consequence of the language acquisition process. These actions can result in the placement of students in special education who do not truly have LD. On the other hand, some practitioners may be fearful of referring ELLs into special education because they believe it is wrong to refer students before they are fully proficient in English, or they might assume that a student's struggles are due to language acquisition when in fact the student does have LD. When this happens, students who have LD go without services and continue to struggle with the general education curriculum. These different kinds of inappropriate decisions characterize the complexities of disproportionate representation among ELLs.

THE EVOLVING LEARNING DISABILITIES CATEGORY

What are learning disabilities? Over the past four decades, definitions of LD and terminology have evolved (see Table 1.2; Gallego, Duran, & Reyes, 2004). After more than 40 years of discussions and advocacy, the field of LD continues to struggle to develop an operational (working) definition.

The origin of the LD definition lies in the traditional medical model of disabilities. The field has considered LD a condition needing diagnosis that is centered within the child rather than in the educational environment (Doris, 1993). This model is a deficit-based approach (Gallego, Zamora-Duran, & Reyes, 2004). In the early 1960s, Samuel Kirk (1962) coined the term "learning disability." Bateman (1965) was dissatisfied with Kirk's definition and developed a different one that was the first to refer to an IQ-achievement discrepancy. This was the beginning of 40 decades of implementation of the IQ discrepancy-based model, which classified students with LD based on a significant difference between potential and actual academic performance.

At the time, the model was validated by Rutter and Yule's (1975) research, which classified two types of impaired readers based on associations between IQ (potential) and achievement (actual performance). In other words, Rutter and Yule found a cluster of impaired readers at the low end of the scale who seemed to share common characteristics and could be categorized as having reading disabilities because they demonstrated significant discrepancies between expected and observed reading scores. The researchers defined the second type of impaired reader as having "general reading backwardness." These students did not demonstrate a discrepancy between expected and observed reading skills but instead exhibited general learning problems. Years later researchers determined that Rutter and Yule's research was flawed, and there had appeared to be a cluster of impaired readers because of problems with testing procedures (e.g., Stuebing et al., 2002). In fact, students' reading and IQ scores fall along a continuum—there is no cluster at the bottom of the scale.

Table 1.2   Historical Timeline of Key LD Definitions

- 1962 Samuel Kirk: A learning disability refers to a retardation, disorder, or delayed development in one or more of the processes of speech, language, reading, writing, arithmetic, or other school subject resulting from a psychological handicap caused by a possible cerebral dysfunction and/or emotional or behavioral disturbances. It is not the result of mental retardation, sensory deprivation, or cultural and instructional factors. (Kirk, 1962, p. 263)
- 1965 Barbara Bateman: Children who have learning disorders are those who manifest an educationally significant discrepancy between their estimated potential and actual level of performance related to basic disorders in the learning process, which may or may not be accompanied by demonstrable central nervous system dysfunction, and which are not secondary to generalized mental retardation, educational or cultural deprivation, severe emotional disturbance, or sensory loss. (Bateman, 1965, p. 220)
- 1977 U.S. Department of Education: The term "specific learning disability" (SLD) means a disorder in one or more of the psychological processes involved in understanding or in using language, spoken or written, which may manifest itself in an imperfect ability to listen, speak, read, write, spell, or do mathematical calculations. The term does not include children who have LD that are primarily the result of visual, hearing, or motor handicaps, or mental retardation, or emotional disturbance, or of environmental, cultural, or economic disadvantage. (U.S. Office of Education, 1977, p. 65,083)
- 1981 National Joint Committee on Learning Disabilities: Learning disabilities is a generic term that refers to a heterogeneous group of disorders manifested by significant difficulties in the acquisition and use of listening, speaking, reading, writing, reasoning, or mathematical abilities. These disorders are intrinsic to the individual and presumed to be due to central nervous system dysfunction. Even though a learning disability may occur concomitantly with other handicapping conditions (e.g., sensory impairment, mental retardation, social and emotional disturbance) or environmental influences (e.g., cultural differences, insufficient/inappropriate instruction, psychogenic factors), it is not the direct result of those conditions or influences. (Hammill, Leigh, McNutt, & Larsen, 1981, p. 336)
- 1997 & 2004 Individuals with Disabilities Act (IDEA): The term "specific learning disability" means a disorder in one or more of the basic psychological processes involved in understanding or in using language, spoken or written, which disorder may manifest itself in imperfect ability to listen, think, speak, read, write, spell, or do mathematical calculations.
  - **Disorders Included**—Conditions such as perceptual disabilities, brain injury, minimal brain dysfunction, dyslexia, and developmental aphasia.
  - **Disorders Not Included**—Learning problem that is primarily the result of visual, hearing, or motor disabilities, of mental retardation, of emotional disturbance, or of environmental, cultural, or economic disadvantage. (IDEA Amendments of 1997, Sec. 602(26), p. 13)
  - IDEA 2004 maintains the SLD definitions found in IDEA 1997 and earlier versions of the law; however, it seeks to update and improve the criteria for SLD identification and eligibility by eliminating the requirement that students must exhibit a severe discrepancy between achievement and intellectual ability in order to be found eligible for services under IDEA (regardless of age). Instead, states may consider how a student responds to research-based interventions when making eligibility determinations.

In 1975, Congress passed PL 94-142, the Education for All Handicapped Children Act (EAHCA). This is the precursor to the Individuals with Disabilities Education Act (IDEA; 1991, 1997, 2004). However, it was not until 1977 that the U.S. Office of Education put forth a definition of LD (see Table 1.2). This conceptual definition became the most commonly used in the United States' public education system. It is important to note that the federal government never explicitly or clearly explained the LD definition or stated how to operationalize it to identify children for special education. Thus, they left state and local educational agencies to figure this out on their own. Rather, the federal government assumed that the definition would provide a theoretical framework for use in identification (Hallahan & Mercer, 2002). Since the initial passage of EAHCA in 1975, intermittent amendments have passed without any major changes to the LD definition. This lack of clarification and difficulties reaching consensus continue to pose challenges in developing LD identification criteria (Gallego, Zamora-Duran, & Reyes, 2004).

In 1978, several major LD professional organizations along with the Adults and Children with Learning and Developmental Disabilities Organizations (ACLD) formed the National Joint Committee on Learning Disabilities (NJCLD) to attempt to provide a united front in addressing issues pertaining to LD (Hallahan & Mercer, 2002). In 1981, NJCLD put forth its own definition of LD (see Table 1.2). Notably there was no mention of psychological processes in this definition. The committee omitted this because of negative reactions to the perceptual-motor training programs in the field at that time (Gallego, Duran, & Reyes, 2004).

Reformation efforts continued through the 1980s by various organizations that were unhappy with the federal definition. At the same time, the U.S. Department of Education continued to fund studies to solidify the federal definition and develop effective methods for identification based on it. Despite NJCLD's strong position and the popularity in some circles of their alternative definition, the federal LD definition remained intact with the reauthorization of the Individuals with Education Act of 1997.

As the new millennium began, the IQ-discrepancy criteria were under increasing scrutiny. In 2001, the U.S. Office of Special Education Programs (OSEP) sponsored the LD Initiative Summit to discuss various aspects of LD (Gallego, Duran, & Reyes, 2004). The purpose of this summit was to develop an LD research synthesis that could provide useful information mainly to practitioners when making decisions concerning identifying students with LD. There were eight major points generated at this summit. As shown in Table 1.3, the results from the summit indicated that the discrepancy-based model was insufficient and ineffective for identifying students with LD and that further research needed conducting on the discrepancy-based model in order to verify its validity (Gallego, Duran, & Reyes). When Congress reauthorized the Individuals with Disabilities Education Improvement Act in 2004, the LD definition remained the same. However, the law did incorporate the Summit's recommendations regarding LD identification procedures. By far the most dramatic change was the elimination of the requirement that a student show a severe discrepancy between intellectual ability and academic achievement in order to qualify as having LD.

Table 1.3   Learning Disability Initiative Summit: Eight Major Consensus Statements

1. Concept of Specific Learning Disabilities (SLD)—Research evidence supports the validity of SLD as an intrinsic disorder of learning and cognition—"LD is not socially constructed."

2. Students with an SLD have the right to receive special education and related services at no cost.

3. SLD is lifelong condition—Students' needs with SLD extend beyond the classroom.

4. SLD prevalence is unknown—However, 6 percent of students receive instruction and resources that require special education.

5. Continued discrepancy between IQ and achievement—There are opposing arguments on this issue. However, the majority opinion supports that a discrepancy is unnecessary and insufficient for identifying LD. The minority opinion supports the discrepancy-based model for identifying LD, but they believe it is not sufficient to verify underachievement.

6. Processing deficits—Some deficits have been linked to SLD.

7. Effective Interventions—Effective interventions for SLD students are effective with consistency, appropriate intensity, and fidelity.

8. Response to Intervention (RTI)—Alternative methods must be developed to identify students with SLD. RTI is an alternative model that is the most promising method of alternative identification that can also promote effective school practices and help close the gap between identification and treatment.

The LD Definition and ELLs

The characteristics of LD and second language acquisition can appear quite similar. For this reason, practitioners have assessed and diagnosed many ELLs as having LD when they may not have actually had disabilities. Over the years, a growing number of ELLs have met the requirements for LD. Yet the LD definition and identification criteria have not adequately taken into account students' linguistic and sociocultural differences, limiting their usefulness with ELLs (Gallego, Duran, & Reyes, 2004).

Presently, many practitioners continue to look for a discrepancy between achievement and intellectual ability in one or more areas related to language processing skills when determining placement into special education. On one side, many practitioners believe that the discrepancy-based model is the foundation of the LD diagnosis, while on the other side many practitioners favor a more ecologically based identification process.

Many researchers and practitioners question if assessment and identification practices take into account students' cultural and linguistic backgrounds (Gallego, Duran, & Reyes, 2004). As long as federal regulations do not specify how to identify LD in ELLs and states must design their own LD identification criteria, practitioners will struggle with identification procedures. Because LD identification criteria vary widely from state to state, a student may be LD in one state but not in another. These challenges are compounded when the student is an ELL.

WHAT WE KNOW FROM RESEARCH ON ELLS WITH LD

Klingner, Artiles, and Mendez-Barletta (2006) reviewed and summarized research on ELLs who struggle with reading and who may have LD. They wanted to find out what we know from research about how to differentiate between ELLs who are struggling because they are not yet fully proficient in English and ELLs who have actual LD. Their goal was to develop recommendations for practitioners.

Research indicates that language acquisition is a complicated process influenced by many factors, including but not limited to the sociocultural environment, language proficiency in the first language, attitudes, personality, and perceived status of the native language in comparison with English. They found that cultural conflict and affective considerations such as motivation appear to be of critical importance when considering why students might be struggling, but that practitioners often overlook these factors. Behaviors that appear to indicate LD might be normal for the child's cultural background or be a by-product of the acculturation process. Practitioners involved in referral and placement decision making should consider various characteristics in relation to a child's culture, language, and acculturation. Similarly, they should consider the learning context when considering why a student is not thriving.

Research also suggests that in many cases psychologists and others involved in evaluating ELLs for possible special education placement tend to ignore or give insufficient attention to the native languages of the children they are testing. They often use English language tests even when a student's background warrants bilingual testing, and tend not to consider whether the unexpected underachievement of ELLs can be explained by their limited English proficiency.

Factors that correlate with later reading achievement in English, or in the student's native language, include phonological awareness, print awareness, and alphabetic knowledge. Rapid naming also plays a role. These early predictors of reading show promise for identifying ELLs who may benefit from additional literacy instruction in the general education environment before referring them to special education, as in an RTI model.

The most promising early intervention programs seem to be those that combine phonological awareness and other reading activities with ESL strategies. Native language support is also beneficial. Other promising practices focus on teaching ELLs reading comprehension strategies.

Klingner et al. (2004) found that more and less proficient readers differ from each other in significant ways. Struggling readers focus more on surface aspects of reading, use fewer comprehension strategies, tap less into background knowledge, and have more limited vocabularies. Yet, importantly, they are able to transfer strategies from their native language to English reading. Also noteworthy is that standardized reading tests may underestimate what ELLs know and can do.

More research is still needed to help us better understand how ELLs with and without disabilities differ as they become bilingual and biliterate. By understanding the characteristics of subpopulations of students with different profiles, the educational community could develop better identification tools and procedures to address disproportionate representation and more accurately determine which students are most likely to benefit from special education services.

CONCLUSION

Practitioners who educate ELLs continue to face challenges as the field of LD struggles to (a) establish an acceptable definition; (b) clarify conceptual and operational frameworks for developing adequate assessments and interventions, particularly for ELLs; and (c) transition from a discrepancy-based identification approach to an RTI model. Although the research base on ELLs who struggle with reading is incomplete, practitioners can still learn much that can inform decisions about how best to assess and teach ELLs. It is through these efforts that ELLs who struggle to read will receive appropriate instruction and inappropriate referrals and placement into special education will be reduced.

2 Misconceptions About the Second Language Acquisition Process

Janette K. Klingner, Estella Almanza de Schonewise, Carmen de Onis, and Laura Méndez Barletta

Certainly one of the biggest challenges teachers of English language learners (ELLs) face is trying to figure out the extent to which a student's struggles can be attributed to the second language acquisition process. Few teachers have obtained advanced degrees in second language acquisition; thus, it is not surprising that they have many misconceptions about how students acquire a new language. A variety of factors contribute to current misconceptions, including a lack of understanding that ELLs' level of educational success is very much a negotiation between what they bring to their schooling and what schools offer them. Schools that are not prepared for an influx of culturally and linguistically diverse students may not have appropriate materials and programs in place, or enough well-prepared teachers ready to build on students' strengths and meet their needs. Also, teachers' confusions about linguistic and literacy development in a second language tend to contribute to a deficit view of the learning potential of ELLs. When ELLs do not seem to be progressing quickly enough, teachers may consider the "problem" to be that they do not speak enough English. One frustrated teacher exclaimed, "Why can't these kids just learn to speak English?" (Orosco, 2007, p. 156).

There is a great deal of natural variation in the language acquisition process. By gaining a greater understanding of this variability, practitioners are better able to support students' learning and advocate for their students. Our objectives in this chapter are to help teachers understand potential misconceptions about the language acquisition process and learn ways to address these misconceptions so that they can enhance their instruction and reduce inappropriate referrals to special education.

Numerous insights can be found in the research literature about the second language acquisition process (Baca & Cervantes, 2004; Collier, 2005; Cummins, 1986, 1989; Figueroa, 1989; Ortiz & Maldonado-Colon, 1986; Ruiz, 1988, 1989). Our goal is to draw from this literature to offer educators positive and constructive solutions to the challenges they face in their schools and classrooms with students who are in the process of becoming bilingual and bi-literate. We list misconceptions and corresponding realities in Table 2.1, and then elaborate about each misconception in the remainder of the chapter.

MISCONCEPTION 1

Bilingualism means equal proficiency in both languages.

Bilingualism is a unique characteristic shared by many ELLs with and without special needs and one that continues to be misunderstood by the education community at large. ELLs in our public school system include children who are foreign born as well as those native to the United States. The language proficiencies that ELLs bring to their schooling are different from those of monolingual English speakers. ELLs' linguistic proficiencies are the *sum* of their proficiencies in their different languages. Variation also exists in the linguistic proficiencies among ELLs. ELLs vary in how proficient they are in their home language as well as in English.

The process of language acquisition is dependent on the cultural and linguistic environments to which students have been exposed (Valdés & Figueroa, 1994). As discussed previously, some immigrant children arrive as newborns or before formal schooling age. Other immigrants arrive at school age, some with and some without formal schooling in their native country. Other ELLs are born in the United States of recent immigrant parents, representing a first, second, or third generation. It is important to acknowledge that ELL backgrounds vary, and consequently a variety of linguistic proficiencies in native languages and English are represented within this broad group.

ELLs by definition are speakers of a language other than English who are in the process of acquiring English proficiency. Many ELLs enter schooling as emergent bilinguals in both languages, with some degree of proficiency in two languages. These students are referred to as

Table 2.1   Misconceptions and Realities

Misconception	Reality
Bilingualism means equal proficiency in both languages.	Bilingualism rarely means equal proficiency in both languages—ELLs' backgrounds and linguistic proficiencies in the native language and English vary.
Semilingualism is a valid concept and non-non classifications are useful categories.	Semilingualism and non-non categories are the results of tests that do not measure the full range and depth of students' language proficiencies.
Native language assessments present a clear picture of linguistic proficiency.	Commonly used native language proficiency assessments provide a limited view of ELLs' oral language proficiency.
Literacy instructional frameworks developed for monolingual students are appropriate for developing ELLs' literacy skills in their native or second language.	Literacy instruction in a second language differs in key ways from native language instruction; a different framework is needed.
The more time students spend receiving English instruction, the faster they will learn it.	Students who receive some native language instruction achieve at higher levels in English than students who do not receive any native language instruction.
All ELLs learn English in the same way at about the same rate.	The length of time it takes students to acquire English varies a great deal, from four to seven years or more. There are many different variables that affect the language acquisition process.
English language learners acquire English in the same way they acquire their first language, through exposure and interactions with others.	Exposure to English and interactions with others are important, but they are not enough to provide the support ELLs' need to be able to fully participate in classroom learning and achieve to their potential; explicit instruction at an appropriate level helps.
Errors are problematic and should be avoided.	Errors are a positive sign that the student is making progress, and are a necessary aspect of second language acquisition. Errors provide clues about a student's interlanguage.

"simultaneous" bilinguals, where exposure to two languages occurs early in life. Students who enter school as monolingual in their native language are referred to as "sequential" bilinguals. When sequential bilinguals enter public school, they quickly begin to negotiate two languages. Both routes involve the process of bilingualism (Escamilla & Escamilla, 2003; McLaughlin, 1984).

In simple terms, *bilingualism* can be defined as knowing two languages rather than one. Valdés and Figueroa (1994) noted that a commonly held view ascribes bilingualism "only [to] those able to function as native speakers of each of their two languages" (p. 7). However, they disagree with this view, and point out that very few individuals actually achieve a state of bilingualism in which both languages reach native-like proficiency levels. In reality, bilingualism rarely means equal proficiency in both languages.

The variability of contexts in which children are immersed influences children's exposure to language, and as a consequence, the development of linguistic proficiency in each language. Homes and schools are rarely balanced environments. Language and knowledge are gained in different domains, for different functions, not necessarily in the same domains or functions in both languages (Escamilla & Escamilla, 2003; Valdés & Figueroa, 1994). In other words, a student may know science terms better in English than Vietnamese because he has been taught in English in school, but know more everyday language in Vietnamese.

Valdés and Figueroa (1994) emphasize the complex and multifaceted nature of bilingualism, advocating for a broader definition of bilingualism as "a common human condition in which an individual possesses more than one language competence [. . .] that makes it possible to [. . .] function at some level in more than one language" (p. 8). This definition places an emphasis on "more than one language" and "competence and ability" to function in more than one language. These qualifiers may seem obvious; however, at present the educational community at large generally fails to validate the *native* language ability ELLs bring to their schooling. In U.S. schools, starting kindergarten knowing only one language is the norm, whereas knowing more than one language is somehow deviant. Rather than seeing ELLs as potential bilinguals, they are defined as "limited" in English. Yet, what if we considered it the norm to know more than one language (as it is in many countries)? Then those who only speak one language would be considered "limited."

Implications for Practitioners

1. ELLs include students with a wide range of proficiencies in their native language and English.

2. Bilingual students may be stronger in some areas in their native language and stronger in other areas in English.

3. Students who begin school proficient in a language other than English are potential bilinguals.

MISCONCEPTION 2

Semilingualism is a valid concept and "non-non" classifications are useful categories.

The language variety that ELLs bring to school in their native language is often deemed as "low" level, particularly among children from low-income families. MacSwan (2004) points to flaws in theories and assessment practices that characterize minority students as "non" speakers in their native language and English. Bilingual development differs from monolingual development, and yet assessment tools typically utilize monolingual speakers as a point of reference. The process of becoming bilingual is complex for ELLs with and without special needs. Yet assessments rarely capture this complexity. In order to identify anomalies in the language acquisition process (i.e., determine which students may have a true language delay), accurate "norms" of bilingual development need to be understood. One of these norms includes how we classify students who are bilingual.

When we categorize children as "limited English proficient" (LEP), we evoke particularly negative connotations for them. The term LEP was coined by Congress in section 9101 of the Elementary and Secondary Education Act of 1965 and continues to be used for legislative purposes. While this term serves the purpose of identifying students who are in need of educational assistance based on their linguistic status and appropriating funding for such programs, unfortunately, it also establishes a "limited" mindset toward ELLs in the United States, which permeates our society. Concerns about the negativity of the LEP label have long been iterated by many in the educational community (Crawford, 1999; MacSwan, 2004; Ovando, Collier, & Combs, 2003). Labels such as "potentially English proficient," "linguistically and culturally diverse," and "English language learners" are meant to be more positive and have evolved from opposition to the negative view that the label LEP ascribes to individuals who speak a native language other than English.

MacSwan (2004) addresses the pervasive deficit view of language minority students in the educational field (e.g., MacSwan & Rolstad, 2003; MacSwan, Rolstad, & Glass, 2002) and challenges the widely accepted view of many English language learners as "non-nons" (i.e., classifying such children as limited in both English and their native language; MacSwan & Rolstad, 2003, p. 1). MacSwan refers to the 6,800 children classified by the Los Angeles Unified School District as non-nons, as reported by *The Los Angeles Times* (1996) as a case in point. MacSwan (2000) argues that "it is unnecessary and insufficient" to characterize the language many English language learners bring to school as low level and lacking, for academic and social-political reasons (p. 15). MacSwan attributes this non-non "crisis" to the widely accepted construct of "semilingualism," arguing that the acceptance of this condition so frequently ascribed to language minority students in the United States propagates a widespread deficit orientation, ultimately setting in place a self-fulfilling prophecy for their academic failure.

"Semilingualism" is identified as a type of bilingualism characterized by "low level [ability] in both languages" in the Threshold Hypothesis (Cummins, 1979, p. 230). Cummins (1981) replaced semilingualism with the term "limited bilingualism." However, theoretically the two terms refer to the same notion (MacSwan, 2000). Bilinguals with low levels of language development are placed in the "lower threshold of bilingual competence" (MacSwan, p. 230). This is in contrast to more advanced levels of bilingualism, "dominant bilingualism," and "additive bilingualism," which refer to native-like ability in one language and high levels in both languages, respectively (p. 230). Negative cognitive effects are associated with *limited* bilingualism (semilingualism), neutral cognitive effects with *dominant* bilingualism, and positive cognitive effects with *additive* bilingualism.

At a fundamental level, MacSwan (2000) refutes semilingualism. He asserts that language minority students come to school with language variation that in and of itself is rich, complex, and fully evolved, challenging the characterization of the language variation by masses of language minority students in both their native language and English brought to public schools at a low level. MacSwan cites studies by linguists, which universally find that children by the age of 5 or 6 have acquired the language of their community (Chomsky, 1965; Gleitman & Landau, 1994; Pinker, 1994). MacSwan asserts that research on preschool language development shows that when children begin school they have "acquired most of the morphological and syntactic rules of their language" (Tager-Flusberg, 1997, p. 188) and "possess a grammar essentially indistinguishable from adults" (MacSwan, 2004, p. 4). The reason these ELLs appear limited is that language assessments do not adequately measure the full range of students' linguistic skills.

The language of minority students, in their native language and English, may vary from monolingual norms; however, their language is still fully viable and evolved. MacSwan (2000) concurs with Cummins that language variation does in fact exist. However, MacSwan advocates that this language variation not be viewed as differences in language *ability*. He notes that attributing "negative cognitive effects" to a supposed lower threshold level of bilingual competence brings social and political disadvantages to language minority populations in the United States. MacSwan (2000) asserts, "If teachers believe that some children have low language ability in both languages, then this belief may have a strong negative effect on their expectations for these children and the curricular content and teaching practices students receive" (p. 6).

Implications for Practitioners

1. The vast majority of children begin school having acquired the morphological and syntactic rules of their language.

2. Current language assessment measures rarely capture the full range of skills that bilingual children bring to the classroom. This inadequate understanding of bilingual children's skills and abilities can contribute to low expectations for ELLs.

3. Classifying students as "low-lows" or "non-nons" is not useful because it does not guide teachers as to what students know or need to learn; rather, it encourages teachers to have low expectations for these students.

MISCONCEPTION 3

Native language proficiency assessments commonly administered to ELLs to determine their native language proficiency present a clear picture of linguistic proficiency.

As discussed above, native language testing of ELLs is problematic because it is used to legitimize a deficit orientation toward ELLs by falsely identifying them as non-speakers at a high rate (MacSwan, 2000, 2004; MacSwan, Rolstad, & Glass, 2002). MacSwan and colleagues point out that there are numerous flaws in the test construction and validity of the commonly administered native language assessments used to justify semilingualism and non-non labels. For example, there are several anomalies in the Pre-Language Assessment Scales Oral—Español (LAS-E) that must be examined against the background of several decades of credible research on language acquisition. They concur with Valdés and Figueroa (1994), who articulated the need to critically examine the practice of native language testing, given that bilingual students do not fit monolingual norms due to the nature of bilingualism.

One problem with some native language tests used in the United States is that although they are intended to assess children's oral language ability, they also tap into other literacy skills. To avoid labeling non-literates as semilingual or alingual, we should carefully distinguish between *oral* language, an integral part of every person's identity, and *written* language, used by some but not all individuals and human societies. Some test makers include items on their oral language instruments that assess aspects of language use that are specific to academic culture—and, in some cases, items or subparts that are not specifically related to language ability at all. Doing so in the context of oral native language assessment, and characterizing the results as an index of native language ability, leads to false impressions about students' potential and privileges the educated classes (MacSwan & Rolstad, 2003).

MacSwan (2004), MacSwan, Rolstad, and Glass (2002), and Valdés and Figueroa (1994) all recommend abandoning the routine practice of testing language minority students' oral native language. After all, they note, the oral language proficiency of native English speaking children is only assessed when a disability is suspected, not as regular practice. They suggest that decisions of program placement and identification for language services can be done with home language surveys, brief parent interviews, and a second language assessment. Falsely identifying ELLs as non-speakers of their native language and English stands to do more harm than good in the educational services these students receive.

Research to Practice

MacSwan (2004) examined the results of the Language Assessment Scales Oral–Español (LAS-E; De Avila & Duncan, 1990, 1994), the Spanish Idea Proficiency Test I (IPT), and the Woodcock-Muñoz (WM), administered to approximately 160 children, ages 6 to 8, with a Spanish-speaking background who had recently scored "non" on the English version of the LAS-E. The research team elicited natural speech samples from participants by asking them to tell a story while looking at a wordless picture book about a boy and a frog (Mayer, 1969), in both Spanish and English. They then coded the speech samples for "lexical, morphological, and syntactic structures and errors as is standard in work on child language and language impairments" (MacSwan, 2004, p. 5).

MacSwan (2004) compared the results of the analysis of the natural language samples with the results on the formal native language assessments and found that the children scored at various levels of proficiency on the LAS-E, IPT, and WM, whereas little variation was found on the natural language samples in the rate of error in morphology and syntax in Spanish. The LAS, IPT, and WM identified large numbers of children as non-speakers or as limited in their native language, but the Spanish language samples showed that all but two students showed no more than an 11 percent morphological error rate, with 94 percent of the students having a 5 percent or less error rate. These children showed a mean morphological error rate well below the mean rate for normally developing children as found by Reilly, Bates, and Marchman (1998). The error rate for one child was found to be extraordinarily high, which may suggest language impairment. MacSwan concluded that the evidence from the natural language samples showed that the children in this study had learned the language of their community even though many of them were identified as "non" speakers of their native language using standardized tests.

Implications for Practitioners

1. The routine practice of administering formal assessments of students' native language proficiency should be abandoned.

2. Widely used native language proficiency assessment instruments may yield invalid results that could lead to inappropriate educational services.

3. Other forms of authentic assessment should be used to determine language proficiency levels of ELLs, including natural language samples.

MISCONCEPTION 4

Literacy instructional frameworks that were developed for monolingual students are appropriate for developing bilinguals' literacy skills in their native or second language.

While there are some aspects of "good teaching" in general that transfer to "good teaching" for English language learners, effective instructors also know that there are important differences between native English learners and bilingual learners, and they capitalize on these to enhance student learning. For example, benchmarks for student development differ for bilinguals as compared to monolinguals (Davidson, 1999). They also differ for younger as opposed to older English language learners because primary and secondary level students tend to develop bilingualism differently. For instance, high school students may need to build vocabulary but are more likely than primary students to understand many components of grammar already, based on prior native language instruction about grammar that transfers to their second language (Garcia, 1998; Jiménez, 1997). In addition, within groups of bilinguals, some may develop oral and written language in a parallel fashion at the same time, while others may develop one mode of language, such as writing, faster than another, such as speaking.

An additional difference between teaching ELLs and native English speakers is that ELLs have learned some principles of language that will transfer to English. Yet students may not automatically recognize these. Studies demonstrate that linguistic elements that do transfer from students' native languages to English should be explicitly taught to help students understand the connections between their native language(s) and English (August & Shanahan, 2006). Teachers would be wise to find out which linguistic elements do not transfer so they can target instruction to meet the needs of their particular students. These linguistic elements will vary depending on which native languages students speak and how similar or dissimilar they are to English. Some schools serve speakers of many languages and it may be difficult to teach to all of the similarities and differences between all the languages and English. However, in many schools the majority of ELLs come from Spanish speaking backgrounds, so schools would be wise to invest in educating teachers to at least teach to the similarities and differences between Spanish and English.

One example of a "best practice" that is not always "best" for ELLs is the process approach to writing instruction. Reyes (1991) found that process approaches that worked well in general for native English speakers, such as literature logs and dialogue journals, were not successful for ELLs unless teachers made specific modifications for these students. Ferris and Hedgecock (1998) noted that second language learners may have different understandings of how to paraphrase or include citations to others' work, and they may have had limited experience with peer reviewing, revising, and teachers' indirect forms of feedback, such as the use of questions or suggestions rather than directives (e.g., "Have you considered saying this a different way?" rather than "Say this is a different way."). Therefore, ELLs benefit from more direct instruction in these areas in order for process approaches to serve them adequately (Harper & de Jong, 2004).

Another practice that is commonly part of writing instruction that may work with native English speakers, but not with ELLs, is to ask students to notice what sounds "right" or "best." This generally will not meet ELLs' needs because they have not learned enough English to develop intuitions about aspects of English writing such as spelling or grammar.

Teachers who are well-informed about students' native language and how they have learned literacy in the past can use this knowledge to scaffold students' learning in English. Aspects that are useful to be aware of include "cross-linguistic differences at the phrase, sentence, and discourse levels (e.g., basic differences in word order at the phrase or sentence level, or differences in purpose and position of a topic sentence at the paragraph level)" (Harper & de Jong, 2004, p. 157). See Chapter 4 for information about ways reading instruction should differ for ELLs.

Research to Practice

Escamilla (2004) examined 110 fourth and fifth grade ELL students' writing samples as well as teachers' evaluations of the writing samples using the Escuela Brillante rubric. Students were native Spanish speakers in an English language acquisition program in Colorado. They had received native language instruction through third grade and most were transitioned to all English instruction by fourth and fifth grades. Two thirds of the teachers were bilingual and one third were monolingual English speakers.

Students wrote one draft responding to a prompt for 30 minutes at the beginning and ending of the school year. Researchers collected 364 writing samples from the 110 students; 64 students wrote only in Spanish, and 46 wrote in both Spanish and English. Using the Escuela Brillante writing rubrics to assess students' writing, teachers first rated some samples independently and then met in groups to arrive at overall ratings and to discuss student writing development and ways to improve writing instruction. After teachers had rated the writing samples, researchers interviewed all teachers about their perceptions of student writing. Researchers also evaluated the writing samples.

The researchers found numerous strengths in students' writing samples, in both Spanish and English. Students conveyed complex ideas and used strong voices. Students' writing demonstrated their deep knowledge of the social and economic realities of their communities, and they were able to generate a number of ideas about how to improve their conditions.

However, teachers' perceptions were negative. Discussions demonstrated a focus on "language as a problem," "bi-illiteracy," and "interference" rather than "transfer" between English and Spanish. Teachers expressed the belief that students were poor writers in both English and Spanish. They believed that students scored low due to (a) being "rushed" into English literacy without having had enough time to fully develop their literacy skills in Spanish, (b) not being taught writing as the focus of school literacy instruction, (c) too much focus on reading and none on writing, and (d) backgrounds (e.g., poverty, limited life experiences) that impeded their writing development. Teachers believed that students' language was a problem and bi-illiteracy was a fact.

The second finding was that rather than looking at students' strengths, teachers focused on students' weaknesses, particularly in writing conventions (e.g., punctuation, use of commas) and organization. In addition, teachers indicated that students lacked background knowledge. Teachers also expressed concern about students' spelling errors, their failure to separate Spanish words (e.g., "alos," "ami," "dela"), and their lack of knowledge of accent marks (Escamilla, 2004). The teachers did not acknowledge the strengths found by the researchers.

The third finding was that teachers attributed writing problems in English to negative transfer, or interference, from Spanish. For example, in the case of one student, teachers observed that one student's spelling issues illustrated her use of Spanish sounds to write English words (e.g., "ticher," "wich," "attencion"). The teachers were concerned with her use of Spanish syntax (e.g., "mad with us") and her failure to hear the ending "s" in English words (e.g., "sometime" and "get," rather than "sometimes" and "gets").

The fourth finding was that teachers were frustrated about their lack of opportunities to develop their own skills in teaching reading and writing in Spanish, as well as teaching emerging biliterate students. Teachers were frustrated that the district provided a plethora of staff development in English literacy instruction; but none of the teachers had ever had an opportunity to attend a staff development session in Spanish around the topic of teaching literacy in Spanish. Furthermore, many teachers described themselves

(Continued)

(Continued)

as limited in knowledge of English and Spanish. For example, many said they did not know how or when to teach accent rules in Spanish literacy; they did not feel comfortable having literary discussions in Spanish; and they did not know how to help develop students' literacy in English as a second language.

The fifth finding was that even though the writing prompts in English and Spanish translated into the same words, they were not equal. They asked students to use the past tense, which in English is simply adding an "ed" to most words; whereas in Spanish the past tense requires accent marks. And the rubric required words with missing or misplaced accents to be counted as misspelled. Therefore Spanish writings were more likely to have errors based on the complexity of the past tense in Spanish. Researchers found that the students' literacy program did not specifically teach students accent rules, despite the fact that they were being assessed on them. One of the major reasons many Spanish writers were deemed marginal was because they lost points due to a lack of knowledge in using accents. Many teachers even indicated that they themselves were unsure of accent rules and how to teach them in Spanish.

Many Spanish speakers in U.S. schools are considered by their teachers to have limited proficiency in English and in their native language. When it comes to writing skills, Escamilla's study found that students' writing samples consisted of complex and sophisticated ideas. Yet these were overlooked by teachers who focused more on language mechanics and looked at students' writing from a deficit perspective. Escamilla cautions that practitioners should avoid the "language as a problem paradigm" and look more clearly at the strengths in students' writing samples (e.g., in terms of expression, ideas, and signs of emerging biliteracy). This will help them move beyond the perception that students are weak writers in both English and Spanish, or bi-illiterate, to an enlightened view of students' emerging biliteracy.

Implications for Practitioners

1. Ongoing professional development can help teachers better understand the ways instruction for ELLs should differ from generic instruction.

2. Many of the perceived writing problems of ELLs are typical of second language learners and should be expected, and are not signs of low levels of development in both languages or of a learning disability.

3. Focusing on students' strengths provides a different picture of what they know and can do than focusing on their errors.

4. ELLs benefit from explicit instruction in ways English is similar to and different from their first language.

MISCONCEPTION 5

The more time students spend receiving English instruction, the faster they will learn it.

This is only common sense, right? After all, we know that time on task increases opportunities to learn and generally enhances academic outcomes. But, counterintuitive though it may be, research shows that a strong foundation in one's native language is more conducive to English acquisition than submersion or immersion in an English only environment (August & Hakuta, 1997). In fact, in their review of research on teaching ELLs to read, August and Shanahan found that some native language instruction led to greater gains in English than no native language instruction (August & Shanahan, 2006). Four previous reviews noted the same thing (Greene, 1997; Rolstad, Mahoney, & Glass, 2005; Slavin & Cheung, 2005; Willig, 1985). In other words, students who are taught using at least some of their native language perform significantly better on standardized tests in English reading than similar students taught only in English. Goldenberg (2006) explained:

> The effects of primary language instruction are modest, but they are real and reliable. The average "effect size" is around .35-.40, depending upon whom is doing the calculation and how it is done (estimates range from about .2 to about .6). Translated, this means that primary language instruction can boost student achievement, in the second language, by about 12–15 percentile points. That's not huge but neither is it trivial. (paragraph 7)

Thus, when teachers support students' use of their first language, they can rest assured that they are helping them and not doing them a disservice (McLaughlin, 1992). Strategic use of the first language, when it is possible, helps ELLs learn grade level content while they are acquiring English, builds a solid foundation that can serve as a bridge to English, and also helps build a bond between the home and the school. Skills developed in the first language transfer to English, particularly when the teacher helps students make connections across languages. Similarly, parents and other caregivers should be encouraged to speak to their children in their home language and engage with them in literacy-related activities in their first language, even when their children are being instructed in English in school (Wong Fillmore, 2000).

One reason that time on task in English by itself is not sufficient for helping students acquire English proficiency, and learn to read, is that instruction must be comprehensible and at an appropriate level to be effective (Krashen, 1981). Krashen explained that ELLs acquire language by hearing messages that are slightly above their current English language level. He referred to this as "Comprehensible Input +1." This is particularly true when the teacher provides scaffolding or support of some kind to help the child make sense of the input (e.g., through gestures, visuals, or simplified language).

Implications for Practice

1. Native language instruction helps students learn English and is more effective than immersion in English only.

2. Skills developed in students' native language transfer to English, particularly when teachers help students make connections across languages.

3. Students acquire English when they receive comprehensible input.

MISCONCEPTION 6

All ELLs learn English in the same way at about the same rate.

Teachers know that not all students learn in the same way, so it would seem obvious that ELLs would differ in how they learn English as a second language. However, many people seem to believe that language learning is a universal process, similar for everyone. Yet, if we think about it, we all know individuals who seem to learn a new language effortlessly, almost by osmosis, and others who really struggle to speak an additional language, despite years of trying. In their summary of the research on ELLs, August and Hakuta (1997) noted, "The most striking fact about second language learning, especially as compared with first language learning, is the variability in outcomes" (p. 37).

There are many reasons the language acquisition process can vary so much. These reasons include the tremendous variability in students' background experiences, the extent to which students have a strong foundation in their first language, how much schooling they have already had, how effective their early literacy instruction has been, and how many opportunities are afforded to them to use their target language in meaningful ways (Cummins, 1986; Portes & Rumbaut, 2001; Valdés, 2001). The child's experiences in the home culture affect values, patterns of language use, and interpersonal styles.

Perhaps one of the most overlooked factors that affects language acquisition is the role of the status of the first language in comparison with that of the majority language, and the attitudes of the society toward the child's first language (Cummins, 2000). If students feel that their language and culture are devalued by their teachers and the general public, they may be less motivated to learn the dominant language of the society. Also, social class differences and cultural differences can contribute to students' sense of safety at and around school, their identity as an English language learner, and thereby their learning of academic English. Children are more likely to be responsive to a teacher who is sensitive to and appreciative of their culture and language.

It takes several years for students to acquire full proficiency in English, longer than many teachers realize. Cummins estimated that it takes five to seven years for students to be able to learn cognitively demanding academic material in their second language (1984). How long it takes seems to vary depending on the nature of the instruction students receive. Garcia (2004) summarized Thomas and Collier's (1998) research, noting:

> It takes typical bilingually schooled students, who are achieving on grade level in L1 (native language), from 4–7 years to make it to the 50th NCE in L2 (English). It takes typical "advantaged" immigrants with 2–5 years of on-grade level home country schooling in L1 from 5–7 years to reach the 50th NCE in L2, when schooled all in L2 in the United States. It takes the typical young immigrant schooled all in L2 in the United States 7–10 years or more to reach the 50th NCE, and the majority of these students do not ever make it to the 50th NCE, unless they receive support for L1 academic and cognitive development at home. (p. 41)

It is important for teachers to keep this in mind because many students appear to be fully proficient in English before they are able to engage with highly demanding, abstract tasks in English. When students struggle, teachers and others may become concerned and suspect that the students have learning disabilities. Or teachers may misinterpret students' behaviors as a lack of motivation. One teacher shared, "I find that these students tend to not understand what I say during instruction. It seems like they are not listening" (Orosco, 2007, p. 157). Yet the most likely explanation for their slow progress is that they are not as fully proficient in English as was thought. This is a common misunderstanding.

Implications for Practice

1. The length of time it takes ELLs to acquire English varies a great deal.

2. Teachers who are aware of students' sociocultural backgrounds can more easily create safe and welcoming environments that affirm students as participants in class and encourage learning.

3. The language acquisition process takes several years; there are no shortcuts.

4. Even when ELLs appear to be quite proficient in English, they may not yet have acquired full proficiency.

5. The reason for an English language learner's struggles when learning to read is much more likely to be the language acquisition process than a learning disability.

MISCONCEPTION 7

English language learners acquire English in the same way they acquire their first language, through exposure and interactions with others.

This misconception is similar to the previous one. Many well-meaning teachers believe that children acquire a second language in much the same way they learn their first language—through exposure and interactions with others in the target language, without the need for direct or explicit instruction (McLaughlin, 1992). Although these conditions are important, by themselves they are not sufficient. And although it is true that the developmental process of learning a second language is similar to that of learning one's first language, there also are important differences that limit the extent to which simple exposure to a new language is effective. For one, children acquiring their first language have many years to do so before they start school. They do not feel the pressure of needing to understand in order to be able to comprehend grade level curriculum, and apply language in complex, often abstract, ways (Swain, 1995). ELLs benefit from conscious attention to their language learning needs, including the grammatical, morphological, and phonological aspects of language (Harper & de Jong, 2004). They need explicit instruction that helps them notice the relationships between the forms and functions of language, and between their first and second languages. Also, teachers must understand that although ELLs may be limited in their ability to express themselves in English, they are *not* limited in their ability to think.

One version of this misconception is the belief that all ELLs develop oral proficiency before they become literate. Yet some students, particularly older ELLs who are already literate in their first language, may actually become proficient with written language before oral language. Interactions with print help them in much the same way oral interactions can help others (Harper & de Jong, 2004). It used to be thought that students should not begin literacy instruction in English until they had developed sufficient oral proficiency in English. And while it certainly is true that students must develop oral proficiency in order to become fully literate, in a recent review of the research on teaching reading to ELLs, Slavin and Cheung (2005) noted that the most effective programs for helping students develop their oral as well as written skills in English are programs in which students learn to read in both languages at much the same time, though at different times during the day. The reason for this is that skills developed in one language transfer to another, particularly when teachers provide explicit instruction and opportunities to practice skills in meaningful ways in both languages.

Implications for Practice

1. The language acquisition trajectories of ELL students are likely to be different from those of monolingual students.

2. Exposure to English and interactions with others are important, but are not enough to provide the support ELLs need to be able to fully participate in classroom learning and achieve to their potential.

3. ELLs benefit from explicit instruction as well as varied opportunities for meaningful practice.

4. Although ELLs may be limited in their ability to express themselves in English, this does not mean they are limited in their ability to think.

MISCONCEPTION 8

Errors are problematic and should be avoided.

Many teachers interpret ELLs' errors in the target language as a sign that they may have a learning disability or a developmental delay (Harper & de Jong, 2004). Yet it is natural for students to make errors while they are learning. In fact, errors are a sign of progress and an indication that students are feeling comfortable enough to take risks. Teachers should keep in mind that ELLs' mistakes often demonstrate the ways in which students are drawing on their native language to help them learn a second language. The process of acquiring a new language includes a stage in which the learner uses an "interlanguage" that includes features of both languages (Selinker, Swain, & Dumas, 1975). This developmental process is obviously different from language development in monolingual English children who do not develop an interlanguage. Errors such as confusion with verb tenses, plurals, possessives, subject/verb agreement, word order, and the use of articles are common (Ferris, 2002; Harper & de Jong, 2004). For example, *"la niña rubia tiene seis años"* in Spanish means "the blonde girl is six years old" in English. However, a literal translation of each word would read, "the girl blonde has six years." A Spanish speaking child who mistakenly says "the girl blonde" rather than "the blonde girl" or "she has six years" rather than "she is six years old" would be transferring knowledge of Spanish to English. This is a normal aspect of second language acquisition, not an indication the child has a language disorder or disability. The kinds of interlanguage errors a child makes vary depending on the characteristics of the first language. In other words, a child who speaks Japanese as his first language will make different errors than a child who speaks Hungarian.

Teachers who are experienced in learning a second language and who know more about the structure of English and other language systems are more likely to understand how students' errors reflect their attempts to make meaning based on their understandings of both their native and target languages. Students benefit when teachers are able to accurately interpret their errors as clues about their language development and provide encouragement and support (Selinker, 1972). Also, teachers should keep in mind that because of some errors' usefulness in students' interlanguages, some mistakes are more or less amenable to correction at different times in students' trajectory of developing proficiency in the target language (Harper & de Jong, 2004).

Many bilingual individuals engage in "code-switching." Code-switching is the practice of combining two languages in one phrase or sentence, or going back and forth between two languages. This is a normal phenomenon and should not be considered an error or sign of confusion (Genesee & Nicoladis, 2006). In fact, code-switching can indicate mastery of two languages rather than that the speaker has limited proficiency in either language. Code-switching is quite common as a sophisticated use of language for social purposes. Lanza (1992) found that children as young as two years old were able to code-switch in socially appropriate ways.

Implications for Practice

1. Errors can be useful clues to understanding the interlanguages that students are developing and can be a sign of progress.

2. Errors such as confusion with verb tenses, plurals, possessives, word order, subject/verb agreement, and the use of articles are common among ELLs and should not be interpreted as signifying that a student has a disability.

3. It is natural that some errors are more amenable to correction than others given their usefulness as part of students' interlanguage.

4. Code-switching is common among bilingual individuals around the world and should not be considered a sign of confusion.

CONCLUSION

ELLs' academic outcomes are greatly influenced by the interactions between what students bring to school and what schooling offers them. We stress the need for well-prepared teachers who understand the language acquisition process and can serve as advocates for their students (Escamilla, 2005). In this chapter, we have discussed eight common misconceptions that can limit the extent to which ELLs receive appropriate instruction and possibly lead to inappropriate referrals to special education.

Harper and de Jong (2004) recommend that, in addition to providing exposure to a language-rich environment and creating opportunities to interact with native speakers of the target language, teachers must also

- ensure that ELLs have the language skills to perform a task, and, if not, teach these skills through explicit modeling and scaffolding
- understand the complex contribution of individual learner variables to the second language acquisition process
- consider a wide range of factors when trying to understand the behaviors of ELLs (i.e., personality, motivation, attitude, educational background, literacy level in the first language, age, and previous opportunities to learn)
- examine the linguistic and cultural assumptions underlying their instructional choices
- attempt to learn more about ways that other cultures structure their children's educational experiences and explore ways that languages are similar and different
- recognize similarities and differences between first and second language learning and understand the implications for their own instructional practices
- understand the role that language plays in learning, and acknowledge that language development must be integrated as a goal of instruction when teaching ELLs
- consider all possible alternative explanations to a student's struggles, including the possibility that instruction might not be appropriate, before thinking that the child might have a learning disability

3 Response to Intervention Models and English Language Learners

Janette K. Klingner, Laura Méndez Barletta, and John J. Hoover

W hat is Response to Intervention (RTI)? When using an RTI model to try and distinguish between learning differences and disabilities among English language learners, what issues are important for practitioners to consider? RTI is a way to provide early intervention to students who show signs of struggling and potentially to identify those who have learning disabilities. RTI offers an alternative to the discrepancy-based identification models of the past that require students to demonstrate a significant gap between their potential, as determined with an IQ test, and their academic achievement, as measured with an achievement test.

RTI holds promise as a way to improve learning outcomes for culturally and linguistically diverse students and reduce their disproportionate representation in special education (Donovan & Cross, 2002). We are particularly encouraged by recommendations to move to a more holistic approach to supporting student learning than has been typical in the past. For example, the National Association of School Psychologists emphasized, "RTI is an approach to evaluate a student's response to an ecological context of instruction and/or intervention" (Christ, Burns, & Ysseldyke, 2005, paragraph 3) and that RTI requires a "shift from a within-child deficit paradigm to an eco-behavioral perspective (and) a greater emphasis on instructional intervention and progress monitoring prior to special education referral . . ." (Canter, 2006, paragraph 7). An emphasis on early intervention, a focus on making sure children receive appropriate instruction at the "first tier" or classroom level, and a push to match instruction to a child's needs based on ongoing classroom assessment are all features of RTI that, when implemented well, should lead to increased opportunities to build reading proficiencies for English language learners. We see potential in the RTI model as a way to help educators shift from finding LD or within-child deficits to focusing on providing the best instruction for all. In this chapter, we provide an overview of RTI, and also discuss some of the challenges schools with high percentages of English language learners (ELLs), such as Marble Mountain Elementary, face when trying to implement RTI.

INTRODUCING RTI AT MARBLE MOUNTAIN ELEMENTARY

Marble Mountain Elementary School has just begun implementing RTI. Their student population is 92 percent Latino (of whom 53 percent are considered English language learners). North County School District selected Marble Mountain as a pilot school for RTI because of concerns about the high percentages of ELLs receiving special education services (31 percent of all ELLs) and the school's low performance on high stakes tests. The district carefully collected the available research about RTI and staff felt confident that they were recommending the most effective and feasible RTI model. They provided three days of professional development to Marble Mountain teachers, support personnel, and administrators on how to implement the various components of RTI. Yet, no sooner had the year begun than the practitioners at Marble Mountain began to experience challenges. We will describe these challenges later in this chapter. But first, we provide an overview of the RTI model.

OVERVIEW OF RTI

RTI is a way of providing intensive support to students who show early signs of struggling. It also is a way of determining who may have learning disabilities. Like common RTI programs around the country, North County School District's RTI model includes certain key components

(National Association of State Directors of Special Education, 2005; Vaughn & Fuchs, 2003):

1. *Providing high-quality instruction/intervention matched to the needs of students.* This type of instruction/intervention has been demonstrated through scientific research and practice to produce high learning rates for students. It is believed that selection and implementation of high-quality instruction/intervention will markedly increase the probability of, but does not guarantee, positive individual response. Results may inform educators about a possible learning disability.

2. *Using students' learning rate over time and level of performance (for ongoing decision making).* Learning refers to a student's growth in achievement or behavior competencies over time compared to prior levels of performance and peer growth rates. Level of performance refers to a student's relative standing on some dimension of achievement/performance compared to expected performance.,

3. *Making important educational decisions.* Decisions about intensity and likely duration of interventions are based on individual student response to instruction across multiple tiers of intervention. Decisions about the necessity for more intense interventions (e.g., eligibility for special education or exit from special education) are based on learning rate and level.

RTI models rely on multiple tiers of intervention, as illustrated in Figure 3.1. The most common model includes three tiers, as we illustrate. Some models, however, include a fourth tier. Whether schools implement a three-tiered or four-tiered model, the last tier is usually special education. This approach incorporates increasing intensities of instruction that are provided to students in direct proportion to their individual needs. Embedded in each tier is a set of support structures or activities that help teachers implement research-based curriculum and instructional practices designed to improve student achievement from which lack of progress may indicate a learning disability (National Association of State Directors of Special Education, 2005).

As shown, students are initially provided evidence-based instruction in Tier 1 and if they do not make adequate progress, or "respond to instruction," supplemental instruction in Tier 2 is provided. For those who continue to experience inadequate progress, Tier 3 or intensive intervention is provided, including special education if necessary. Estimates in the area of reading are that approximately 80 percent of all learners make adequate progress in Tier 1; 15 to 20 percent may require some supplemental instruction in Tier 2, while

Figure 3.1 Three-Tier Model for Response to Intervention

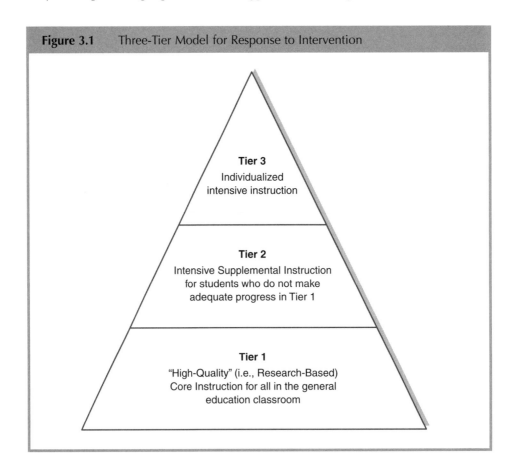

Tier 3
Individualized
intensive instruction

Tier 2
Intensive Supplemental Instruction
for students who do not make
adequate progress in Tier 1

Tier 1
"High-Quality" (i.e., Research-Based)
Core Instruction for all in the general
education classroom

5 percent or less need intensive intervention implemented in Tier 3. The critical components within each tier are illustrated in Table 3.1.

RTI is implemented with students as early as kindergarten. Students who are likely to have reading difficulties are identified and provided interventions that include the critical elements of beginning reading (e.g., phonemic awareness, phonics, fluency, vocabulary, and comprehension). An important component of RTI is the ongoing assessment of a student's proficiency on discrete academic skills, such as phonemic awareness and rapid letter naming. Ongoing assessment is significant because information obtained from assessments informs instruction at each tier and also identifies the appropriate level of service for each student in a timely manner (National Association of State Directors of Special Education, 2005).

Overall, within the RTI process, students who make expected gains are said to "respond" to instruction and are expected to continue to make progress when evidence-based instruction is provided in the general education classroom. Conversely, within RTI, students who make minimal gains after receiving quality, validated interventions are considered to

Table 3.1   Three-Tier Instructional Characteristics

Tiers	Characteristics
Tier 1	• This first tier provides "high-quality" instruction (that is, research-based instruction) to all students within a general education classroom. • Teachers screen students (for example, in literacy skills) to identify levels of proficiency. • Teachers monitor students' progress (using assessments such as the Dynamic Indicator of Basic Early Literacy Skills [DIBELS]). • Students who lag behind on critical measures of performance are identified for additional supports at Tier 2.
Tier 2	• Students who are not making adequate progress (as determined by assessments such as the DIBELS) in the first tier receive supplemental instruction. • Tier 2 is geared toward students who did not "respond" to the intervention provided in the general education classroom. • Tier 2 is still part of general education. • The second tier requires a more intensive, small-group reinforcement of the concepts taught in the general education classroom. • When the second tier of intervention does not adequately meet students' needs, they are considered—based on their lack of response—as being candidates for referral to special education.
Tier 3	• Students who were not "remediated" in the second tier, that is, students who did not "respond" to instruction in Tier 1 or 2, receive specialized support. • Tier 3 is for students who do not "respond" to the small-group instruction and require specialized, intensive instruction, such as that provided by Title I, district remediation programs, or special education programs (National Association of State Directors of Special Education, 2005).

be inadequately responding to intervention (or to be "nonresponders"). According to research (e.g., Fuchs, Mock, Morgan, & Young, 2003), these students may need more intensive long-term interventions (Tier 3), and possibly special education services.

The use of RTI as a means to identify learning disabilities is a new phenomenon. Many proponents of RTI, including researchers, policy makers, and practitioners, believe that it provides a more valid approach to identifying learning disabilities (Hoover, 2006). The premise is that RTI more accurately identifies students as having LD if their academic performance (i.e., reading) does not adequately respond to an implemented intervention. However, some of the assumptions that underlie RTI may be faulty when applied to ELLs. We discuss these next.

ASSUMPTIONS UNDERLYING RTI THAT MAY BE PROBLEMATIC WITH ELLS

RTI is based on certain key principles that can be problematic when applied to ELLs and other culturally and linguistically diverse students (Barrera, 2004; Klingner & Edwards, 2006). When practitioners understand these assumptions, they are in a better position to make wise choices for children and less likely to draw erroneous conclusions prematurely. They realize that there are many possible reasons an ELL might be struggling.

Assumption 1

"Evidence-based instruction" is good instruction for everyone. English language learners who have been taught with generic evidence-based interventions have been provided with sufficient opportunities to learn.

Numerous instructional approaches recommended as being evidence-based (or research-based) have not actually been validated or tried out with ELLs, or in school contexts similar to those in which many ELLs are educated (Klingner & Edwards, 2006). Research can only help us make an educated guess about which practice is most likely to be effective with the majority of students, *not* what practice will work with everyone. In fact, we know that some students learn differently than others—not everyone learns the same. And, students have different learning needs. Vaughn and Fuchs (2003) noted that research on interventions and their efficacy with culturally and linguistically diverse students is very limited. District and school personnel should make every effort to select research-based interventions that actually have been tried, and found to be effective, with students similar to those with whom they will be used. For examples of RTI research conducted with ELLs, see Linan-Thompson, Vaughn, Prater, and Cirino (2004) and Haager (2004; described in this chapter in the Research to Practice Boxes).

Assumption 2

Learning to read in one's second language is similar to learning to read in one's first language; therefore, instructional approaches that have been found through research to be effective with mainstream English speaking students (and thus deemed "research-based") are appropriate for serving ELLs.

Although the developmental processes are similar when learning to read in a first or second language, there also are important differences that must be taken into account when planning for instruction and assessing student progress (see Chapter 4 for a description of these differences; August & Shanahan, 2006). For example, ELLs benefit from additional oral language instruction. Districts and schools should provide professional development in teaching reading to ELLs, and teachers should do all they can to learn about working with this population of students. It is not enough, for example, to have a master's degree in Reading if the graduate program did not include a focus on ELLs (Orosco, 2007).

Assumption 3

Students who fail to respond to research-based instruction have some sort of learning problem or internal deficit, and perhaps even a learning disability.

There are many reasons a child may not respond to a particular instructional approach (Klingner & Edwards, 2006). It could be that the method is not an effective one with this child, and a different approach would yield much better results. Or, the level of instruction might not be a good match for the child. The environment might not be conducive to learning. It is important to look in classrooms and observe instruction, and also to try different approaches, before determining that a child may have a disability because he is not responding to an intervention.

It may be more appropriate to provide ELLs with extra support at the second tier of an RTI model while they are acquiring English rather than placing them in special education.

Research to Practice

Study 1: Researching RTI With English Language Learners

Linan-Thompson, Vaughn, Prater, and Cirino (2004) examined one aspect of the RTI approach for English language learners. They provided "at risk" first grade students with an intervention and then followed them through the second grade. The purpose of the study was to determine how students responded to a comprehensive intervention in comparison with those who received no treatment. This latter group was the "control" students. The researchers assessed students at the end of first grade and then again at the end of second grade. They determined how many of the students who had responded positively to the intervention at the end of first grade maintained that status at the end of second grade. In addition, they calculated the number of students who were still at risk at the end of first grade and continued to be at risk at the end of second grade.

(Continued)

(Continued)

Students received instruction in either English or Spanish, depending on the type of program they were in (i.e., bilingual or immersion) and the language of instruction used by the school. First grade students were screened for reading problems and those most at risk for reading difficulties were randomly assigned to either be a control student or to receive a daily supplemental reading intervention (Linan-Thompson et al., 2004). This was in addition to the instruction they received in the core reading program that all students received, in either English or Spanish. The supplemental reading intervention lasted for seven months, for 50 minutes daily. The lessons included 35 minutes of explicit instruction in phonological awareness, word attack, fluency, comprehension, plus embedded language support for 5 minutes, and story retell for 10 minutes. Students in the control group, on the other hand, received the existing instructional program for struggling learners.

A total of 53 students completed the intervention and were available for testing at the end of first grade. Of the 31 students who received the Spanish intervention, 30 responded to intervention (in other words, showed good progress), and of the 22 students who received the English intervention, 20 responded to it, and 2 did not, suggesting that both Spanish and English interventions were successful by the end of grade one. Across the English and Spanish studies, 40 students completed the intervention at the end of second grade. Of the 40 intervention students who were assessed at the end of first grade, 22 participated in the Spanish intervention and were available for testing at the end of second grade. All 22 students still met "response" criteria at the end of second grade, and would likely not be candidates for referral for special education. A total of 18 students (of the 40 intervention students) participated in the English intervention and were available for testing. Of the 18 students, 17 still met the "response" criteria at the end of second grade, once again indicating the success with both the English and Spanish interventions.

The students in the control groups, on the other hand, did not fare so well. A little more than half of the students, or 30 out of 50, met the RTI "response" criteria (Linan-Thompson et al., 2004) at the end of first grade. Yet, of the students receiving English instruction, only 7 out of 17 students met the criteria. In other words, far more control students than intervention students (in both the Spanish and English studies) did not meet RTI "response" criteria at the end of first grade and were still considered "at risk." Of the 35 students who were available for testing at the end of second grade, 3 students (1 in the Spanish study and 2 in the English study) who had met the study criteria initially were now at risk at the end of second grade.

The findings in this study are striking because they indicate that ELLs at risk for reading disabilities who are provided explicit, systematic, and intensive interventions within general education can make significant gains to the point that they are less at risk for referral to special education. Linan-Thompson et al. concluded that regular classroom instruction is usually insufficient for meeting the literacy learning needs of all ELLs. That is, 91 percent of the students who received the English intervention met the criteria at the end of first grade compared to 41 percent of the students who did not. Students who received only classroom instruction with school-provided supplemental support would be more likely to be referred for special education services than those students who received the comprehensive year-long supplemental intervention. The researchers stated that while it may be labor intensive and expensive to provide a supplemental one year intervention, it is more cost effective and more appropriate than incorrectly identifying students for special education.

Linan-Thompson and her colleagues made another important point. They noted that the students in both the Spanish and English control groups did not meet benchmark standards for reading gains at the same rate as students who received the supplemental treatment intervention. In other words, ELLs needed more time to reach benchmarks. Also, a second year of intensive instruction seemed to be critical, particularly for the students in the English program. They emphasized that English language learners seem to need more time to acquire English skills and additional practice reading than their mainstream counterparts.

Research to Practice

Study 2. Researching RTI With ELLs Through Project PLUS

Haager (2004) implemented an RTI model of prevention and early intervention for improving early literacy outcomes for ELLs who were likely to be identified in later years as having reading-related learning disabilities, calling the program Project PLUS. The researchers provided extensive professional development to school administrators, general education teachers, and special education teachers. They taught teachers how to do progress monitoring using the Dynamic Indicators of Basic Early Literacy Skills (DIBELS; Good & Kaminski, 2002), how to interpret assessment scores, and how to provide intensive support as part of a second tier of reading instruction. Unlike in Linan-Thompson et al.'s (2006) study where the research team provided the Tier 2 support, in Haager's study it was the classroom teachers who provided this assistance within the context of general education reading instruction. In Haager's model, the third tier was considered special education and was provided by special education personnel (Haager, 2004). Haager implemented the three tiers of the RTI model in Project PLUS as follows:

(Continued)

(Continued)

Project PLUS Tiers and Characteristics	
Tiers	*Characteristics*
Tier 1	• Teachers received at least one full week of training in the newly adopted reading program, as well as additional training in English language development methods for English language learners. • Teachers implemented the core program and district required assessments in reading. Teachers assessed their students in basic early reading skills using the DIBELS assessment system. • At the beginning and middle of each academic year, teachers met in grade level groups with research personnel to discuss DIBELS results and identify students who might need Tier 2 intervention.
Tier 2	• Teachers were provided with up-front and ongoing professional development from kindergarten through second grade. • Teachers learned how to analyze assessment data to strategically group students according to areas of need (e.g., phonological awareness, decoding, and fluency). • Teachers learned a set of intervention strategies to implement in small groups focusing on the core areas of beginning reading. • Teachers retaught or pretaught aspects of their core program during small-group intervention sessions. • Teachers integrated English language development instruction into their small-group reading intervention instruction for ELLs. • Teachers met in grade level groups to collaboratively plan how to schedule and implement interventions. • Once or twice a month, teachers planned sessions focused solely on intervention and their struggling readers.
Tier 3	• Special education teachers went into general education classrooms to provide services and follow the progress of students who were identified for Tier 2 intervention. • Special education teachers consulted with classroom teachers regarding intervention techniques, which resulted in Tier 2 students receiving intervention from the classroom teacher and special education teacher. • When it was clear that a student was not responding to an intervention and the classroom teacher made a referral, Tier 3 allowed for the special education teacher to be aware of the student's situation, thereby allowing for the assessment and eligibility process to run smoothly.

IMPLEMENTING RTI AT MARBLE MOUNTAIN ELEMENTARY SCHOOL

The teachers and support personnel at Marble Mountain Elementary School are facing many challenges and seem to have more questions than answers about RTI. They are especially concerned about using RTI with ELLs. Although they are aware that second language acquisition, best practices for ELLs, and cultural variations should be considered when assessing student progress, designing interventions, and interpreting ELLs' responses to interventions, they are not always confident that they have sufficient expertise to carry out these activities. We discuss a few of their challenges next.

Challenge 1

According to progress-monitoring data, more than half of the ELLs in each first grade class are not reaching benchmarks even though they are supposedly receiving research-based instruction. It is not feasible to provide Tier 2 instruction to all of these students.

When many students are not progressing with a particular instructional program, the first step should be to look for ways to make instruction more appropriate for culturally and linguistically diverse students. It is important (a) to examine the program to determine if it has been validated with students like those in the class, (b) to determine whether instruction is at an appropriate level for students and the program is well-implemented, and (c) to establish whether teachers are sufficiently differentiating instruction to meet diverse student needs. Determining how appropriate an instructional program is requires studying the program manual or research reports to find out how the program was developed and tested. What percentage of the students in the original sample (i.e., students who participated in the testing) were English language learners? If the answer is "none," the instructional program is probably not suitable for these students. If the answer is less than half, do the researchers or program developers report how well the English language learners did with the program (separately from other participants)? This is important because researchers can call a practice "effective" if only a small majority of the participants achieve better results with it. It is possible, and in fact, likely, that some students actually did better with a comparison program. What if the students who achieved greater gains with an alternative program were the English language learners? It is important to find this out.

Determining whether a program is well-implemented necessitates observing in classrooms. The program might be an appropriate one, but the teacher may be having trouble applying it with fidelity. Perhaps the teacher is struggling with classroom management and needs assistance in this area before he is able to focus more on instruction. Or perhaps the teacher has not been trained in how to differentiate instruction. It very well could be that the teacher needs more professional development in how to teach reading to ELLs. In Marble Mountain's case, none of the district-provided RTI professional development included this component, and the teachers had not received instruction in teaching reading to ELLs in their teacher education programs. In other words, when so many students seem to be struggling, the first step should be to improve instruction.

Challenge 2

Teachers and other school personnel are not clear how the RTI process is similar to and different from the pre-referral process they had used in previous years. Their RTI meetings look very much like the "child study" team meetings of old.

Teachers' concerns have changed very little—they are still frustrated that their students are not learning more quickly and that they are not receiving more assistance. Discussions at RTI problem-solving meetings still center on possible reasons for a child's struggles from a deficit perspective, in other words, focused on what could be wrong with the child. There still seems to be a push to qualify a student for special education so that he can receive more intensive support. It is natural that it will take time for school personnel to shift their thinking from one of figuring out what is wrong with a student to one of looking more broadly at the instructional context and ways to make it better, as well as at how to provide support for all students who need help, regardless of label. During this transition period, we advise focusing on ways to improve Tier 1 and Tier 2 instruction and interventions to be more appropriate for ELLs, and for all students. Rather than placing a child in Tier 3, we suggest providing a different form of intervention at Tier 2, perhaps for a longer duration, and making sure the instruction is provided by a teacher with expertise in teaching reading to ELLs. Also, see Chapter 5 for more ideas about the similarities and differences between the pre-referral process and the RTI model.

Challenge 3

School personnel are confused about Tier 2 interventions. They wonder (a) whether ELL services "count" as a secondary intervention, and (b) whether a special education teacher can provide Tier 2 interventions.

Tier 2 interventions are only those small-group interventions that are supplemental to the core curriculum and based on students' needs as assessed by universal screening and progress monitoring. Instructional activities designed to support ELLs' English language development should be part of Tier 1, though a multitiered model could be applied for supporting the language acquisition of students who do not seem to be thriving with the Tier 1 instruction they are receiving. Here is a way to think about this: We teach all students how to do mathematics in Tier 1. We teach all students how to read in Tier 1. We should support the English language acquisition of all ELLs in Tier 1. While we are teaching, we should be assessing students' progress. When we find that some students are not progressing well in mathematics, we should provide them with Tier 2 interventions in mathematics; when some students are not progressing well in learning to read, we should provide them with Tier 2 interventions in reading; and when some ELLs are not progressing as we would hope in acquiring English, even though most of their peers are and we have established that the instruction seems to be culturally and linguistically responsive, we should provide them with Tier 2-type interventions in English language acquisition.

Tier 2 is under the domain of general education, *not* special education. Although the special education teacher might serve as a consultant regarding Tier 2 interventions, and may even occasionally provide Tier 2 interventions, particularly if she is modeling how to teach a particular kind of lesson for her colleagues, this should not be her primary role, and she should not be the school's main Tier 2 intervention provider. A general education reading specialist, mathematics specialist, or English language development specialist would be far more appropriate.

Challenge 4

The school has limited resources. School personnel are struggling to figure out ways to make RTI feasible. They lack full sets of books in the basal reading series that they are supposed to be using; they are being asked to pay for and implement progress monitoring in addition to the other high stakes testing they have already been administering; they have one reading specialist providing Tier 2 support, but she does not have time to help teachers with their instruction and also provide intensive instruction for all students who need it; they know their teachers need more preparation in how to work with ELLs and would like to provide more professional development, but cannot afford it.

Schools are part of larger systems. Unless funding structures are changed to provide more support for struggling schools, they are going to find it very hard to implement RTI, or any other reform, for that matter. Marble Mountain's principal has already allocated 15 percent of her special education funding to help pay for the Reading Specialist's salary, as is allowed by the law. She is reallocating Title 1 funds that, in the past, paid for paraprofessionals to fund two additional Intervention Specialists, as well as more materials.

Although the school cannot afford to bring in an external professional developer, the principal allocated resources to provide a small stipend to the one teacher who has a master's degree in teaching culturally and linguistically diverse students. She is facilitating a study group that meets one day a week after school to discuss ELL issues. The principal is now trying to obtain professional development credits for the participating teachers that will contribute to increases on the salary scale. The principal is doing all she can to improve learning opportunities for her school's students, and to make RTI work, but really wishes that she had more guidance in how to do this.

RTI FOR ENGLISH LANGUAGE LEARNERS

Marble Mountain Elementary is not alone in the challenges it faces. To help support Marble Mountain and other schools like it, we developed two tables (see pages 51–56). The first, Table 3.2, was designed to assist school personnel to think about their readiness to implement RTI and what factors should be in place. The second, Table 3.3, provides additional decision points about each tier in the RTI model.

SUMMARY

In this chapter we discussed the emerging practice of RTI relative to the education of ELLs. We provided an overview of the RTI model, discussed assumptions that can be problematic for ELLs, provided examples of two RTI research studies, discussed challenges to RTI implementation, and provided checklists for practitioners to use to help guide their practice. Our intent in this chapter was to provide a foundation for the chapters in this book that follow. Each subsequent chapter provides more in depth information about an aspect of differentiating between learning disabilities and learning differences among ELLs. For example, in Chapter 4 we discuss the different components of reading and how they can present challenges to ELLs. Chapter 5 provides guidelines for reducing bias in decision making by attending to cultural and linguistic factors that may explain suspected learning or behavior difficulties.

Table 3.2   Assessment of School Level Readiness for RTI: Cultural and Linguistic Diversity

Current Schoolwide Reading Practices

Questions	Evidence
1. To what extent have core instructional reading programs been validated with similar students, in similar contexts, taking into account cultural and linguistic diversity?	
2. To what extent does the school's reading program differentiate instruction to meet all students' needs?	
3. To what extent do teachers' practices differentiate instruction to meet all students' needs, given their current levels and rates of reading learning as well as their particular cultural and linguistic needs?	
4. To what extent is instruction targeted to and appropriate for the students' level of English proficiency and learning needs?	
5. To what extent are teachers adequately trained in how to implement the comprehensive, supplemental, and intervention reading programs, particularly with culturally and linguistically diverse students?	
6. To what extent do teachers help students make connections to prior knowledge and to their own experiences?	
7. Does the representation of students who have difficulties or are succeeding in reading match the general representation of students in the school; or are some groups over- or under-represented?	

Current Schoolwide Environment

Questions	Evidence
8. To what extent do teachers demonstrate caring about all students in ways that reflect understanding of students' cultures and languages?	
9. To what extent are teacher-student relationships positive, and expressed in supportive ways?	
10. To what extent is the learning environment supportive, motivating, and meaningful to students?	
11. To what extent are teachers trained in building on the strengths of all students and families in the school, including those who are culturally and linguistically diverse?	

(Continued)

Table 3.2 (Continued)

Current Schoolwide Environment	
Questions	*Evidence*
12. What systems are in place to seek out, welcome, and respond to all families' input on both classroom and school levels in relation to students' reading?	
13. To what extent are the voices of all families in the school heard and considered in a balanced way that is reflective of the student population, rather than some groups being over- or under-represented?	
14. Does the linguistic capacity of school staff meet the linguistic needs of students and families served by the school?	

Current Assessment Practices	
Questions	*Proposed Processes*
15. To what extent does the data management system allow participants to document and analyze both qualitative and quantitative measures of student knowledge and academic progress, in reading as well as other areas?	
16. To what extent are all who are affected by the data management system included in designing a system that addresses their needs, such as core and supplemental teachers, support personnel, paraeducators, administrators, and parents?	
17. To what extent are diverse individuals with expertise in the languages and cultures of the students included in developing the data management system (such as the principal, psychologist, counselor, literacy specialist, special education teacher, ELL specialist, social worker, and one or more classroom teachers)?	
18. Have authentic assessments been used to measure student knowledge and progress in addition to standardized tests?	
19. Do assessments measure what tasks students with difficulties can perform and in what contexts?	
20. How are multiple kinds of assessment data, including standardized as well as informal and observational data, used to inform ongoing instructional decision making?	

Source: Adapted from University of Texas Center for Reading and Language Arts (2003).

Table 3.3   Schoolwide Plan for Improving RTI

Schoolwide Plan for Improving Tier 1 Reading Instruction	
Questions	*Strategic Approaches*
1. Are diverse individuals with expertise in the languages and cultures of the students included in developing the schoolwide plan (such as the principal, psychologist, counselor, literacy specialist, special education teacher, ELL specialist, social worker, and one or more classroom teachers)?	
2. Are representative parents of all students included in developing the plan?	
3. Does Tier I instruction focus on grade-appropriate essential reading components?	
4. Does Tier I instruction focus on the particular linguistic and cultural strengths and needs of students?	
5. Does Tier I instruction differentiate in a way that takes into account all students' levels of reading and rates of progress?	
6. Are most students (including most ELLs) experiencing success with Tier 1 instruction?	
7. How is student progress assessed? How often?	
8. Is a system established for Tier I problem solving and decision making that includes diverse individuals with expertise in the languages and cultures of students affected by the plan?	
9. Through what mechanism are teachers provided with professional development in RTI and in how to meet the needs of culturally and linguistically diverse students? Is assessment used to inform professional development needs?	
10. To what extent does the plan for professional development include experts in students' linguistic and cultural backgrounds, community stakeholders such as parents of all students, and teachers' self-assessment of their needs?	

(Continued)

Table 3.3 (Continued)

Schoolwide Plan for Tier 2 Intervention for Struggling Readers	
Questions	*Strategic Responses*
1. Who will provide Tier 2 intervention (e.g., classroom teacher or specialized reading teacher)?	
2. To what extent will Tier 2 providers have training or expertise in serving culturally and linguistically diverse students?	
3. To what extent will Tier 2 providers have training or expertise in serving struggling readers?	
4. When will Tier 2 intervention be provided (e.g., during centers, before or after school)?	
5. If time is scheduled before or after school, have transportation and other family needs been considered and accounted for to support student participation?	
6. Where will Tier 2 intervention be delivered (e.g., within the general education classroom, in a resource room)?	
7. To what extent will the learning environment for Tier 2 interventions be supportive, motivating, and meaningful to students?	
8. How will Tier 2 providers help students make connections to prior knowledge and to their own experiences?	
9. Is a system in place for frequently monitoring Tier 2 student progress (e.g., every two weeks)?	
10. Does the system for progress monitoring include multiple kinds of measures (both quantitative and qualitative) that assess what students *can* do as well as their needs?	
11. Will experts on students' linguistic and cultural backgrounds be involved in interpreting assessment data and planning instruction?	
12. How will assessment data be used to group and regroup students (small same-ability groups; one-on-one tutoring), to plan targeted instruction, and to make adaptations?	
13. How will parents of all students affected by Tier 2 grouping be included in tracking student progress and changes in interventions?	

Schoolwide Plan for Tier 2 Intervention for Struggling Readers

Questions	Strategic Responses
14. What criteria are established for entry into and exit from Tier 2?	
15. Will the criteria be implemented and reassessed as needed with the help of experts who are knowledgeable about the cultural and linguistic backgrounds and needs of the students involved?	
16. Is a system established for Tier 2 problem solving and decision making?	
17. Will the system be implemented and reassessed as needed in conjunction with experts who are knowledgeable about the cultural and linguistic backgrounds and needs of the students involved?	

Schoolwide Plan for Small Group Tier 3 Intensive Intervention for Struggling Readers With Extreme Reading Difficulties

Questions	Strategic Responses
1. Who will provide Tier 3 intervention (e.g., specialized reading teacher or special education teacher)?	
2. Will Tier 3 providers have training or expertise in serving culturally and linguistically diverse students?	
3. Will Tier 3 providers have training or expertise in serving students with reading difficulties?	
4. Where will Tier 3 intervention be delivered (e.g., within or outside the general education classroom)?	
5. To what extent will the learning environment for Tier 3 intervention be supportive, motivating, and meaningful to students?	
6. How will Tier 3 providers help students make connections to prior knowledge and to their own experiences?	
7. How much additional instructional time for Tier 3 intervention will be scheduled, and when?	
8. If time is scheduled before or after school, have transportation and other family needs been considered and accounted for to support student participation?	

(Continued)

Table 3.3 (Continued)

Schoolwide Plan for Small Group Tier 3 Intensive Intervention for Struggling Readers With Extreme Reading Difficulties	
Questions	*Strategic Responses*
9. Is the relationship of Tier 3 with 504 and special education services determined? Is a system established for Tier 3 problem solving and decision making?	
10. Will the system for problem solving and decision making be implemented and reassessed as needed in conjunction with experts who are knowledgeable about the cultural and linguistic backgrounds and needs of the students involved?	
11. How will assessment data be used to group and regroup students to plan targeted, more intensive instruction, and to make adaptations?	
12. Will experts on students' linguistic and cultural backgrounds be involved in interpreting assessment data and planning instruction?	
13. Will the assessment data include multiple kinds of measures (both quantitative and qualitative) that assess what students *can* do as well as their needs?	
14. How will parents of all students affected by Tier 3 grouping be included in tracking student progress and changes in interventions?	
15. What criteria are established for entry into and exit from Tier 3?	
16. Will the criteria be implemented and reassessed as needed in conjunction with experts who are knowledgeable about the cultural and linguistic backgrounds and needs of the students involved?	
17. Is a system in place for frequently monitoring Tier 3 student progress (e.g., every two weeks)?	
18. Will the system for student monitoring include multiple kinds of measures (both quantitative and qualitative) that assess what students *can* do as well as their needs?	

Source: Adapted from University of Texas Center for Reading and Language Arts (2003).

4 Helping Classroom Reading Teachers Distinguish Between Language Acquisition and Learning Disabilities

Janette K. Klingner and Diana Geisler

The focus of this chapter is on helping classroom teachers distinguish between second language acquisition and learning disabilities (LD) among ELLs by explaining some of the challenges ELLs face when learning to read in English. These challenges can give teachers the false impression that students have LD or lack intelligence when in fact they are simply experiencing normal effects of the language acquisition process. First, let's meet Carole.

Carole teaches first grade at King Elementary School. She has been teaching there for two decades, and over the years has seen the community change from mostly White middle class to predominately Latino working class. Many parents are immigrants and work at the new meat-packing plant nearby. Almost two-thirds of Carole's students speak some Spanish in their homes, and about 40 percent are considered less than fully proficient in English, or, in other words, to be ELLs. King Elementary provides pull out ESL services for their ELLs, for about one hour a day.

Carole earned a master's degree in elementary education during her early years in the classroom, and over the years has been considered an effective teacher by her principal, other teachers, and parents. She is a confident, experienced teacher. Recently she attended district-sponsored professional development workshops on Reading First and the five "big ideas" of reading emphasized in the National Reading Panel report (2000). Like many schools around the country, her district is pushing the use of evidence-based practices. Carole has seen the reading pendulum swing from a focus on whole language to an emphasis on explicit instruction in phonics. She considers herself to be in favor of a balanced approach—something in the middle. She has not taken any coursework or received any professional development in teaching ELLs how to read. She, like those who determine the curriculum in her district, believes that the evidence-based reading practices promoted by the National Reading Panel are appropriate for all students. After all, how much can teaching letter sounds and names vary? She wonders, "Isn't good teaching just good teaching?"

Yet Carole's students are now struggling, and she is not sure why. She believes that, in part, the reason is that her current students are not as prepared for school as were her previous students. Factors related to poverty create additional challenges for them. She sees that not being fully proficient in English creates barriers, and she gets quite frustrated that, despite her best attempts to meet their needs, many of her students simply cannot seem to learn to read. She suspects that a disproportionate number of them might have LD.

Carole is not alone. Teachers often misunderstand students' lack of progress (Orosco, 2007). A common scenario is that a principal or someone in the school district such as the language arts director mandates or recommends using a particular instructional practice, emphasizing that it is research-based.[1] The principal might stress that the practice has been "proven to work." The teacher assumes that because she is using an evidence-based practice, students' struggles must be because something is lacking in the students, not the program. Yet "what works" with some students may not work with *all* students. Most commercially produced curricula in the United States are created to meet the needs of middle-class, native English speakers. They are designed based on assumptions about the cultural and linguistic knowledge this demographic of student brings to the instructional situation. English language learners differ from their mainstream counterparts in significant ways that affect how successful an instructional practice will be (August & Shanahan, 2006).

---

1. Evidence-based and research-based are often used interchangeably to refer to an instructional practice that has been the focus of experimental or quasi-experimental research studies and determined to be more effective than a comparison approach.

In this chapter, we address how classroom teachers can misinterpret ELLs' struggles when they are not responding to instruction as teachers think they should, and then conclude that they might have LD. Most referrals for an evaluation for possible special education placement are made by classroom teachers (Ysseldyke, 2005). And most often, teachers' concerns center on students' lack of progress with reading. Thus, our hope is that if teachers can better understand the reasons for ELLs' struggles, they will be less likely to judge them as deficient.

THE "FIVE BIG IDEAS" OF READING

Although there certainly are many similarities in the best instructional practices for ELLs and students who speak English as their first language, there also are key differences. Recently, to review the research on teaching reading to ELLs, the federal government convened a national panel of experts now known as the National Literacy Panel on Language Minority Children and Youth (August & Shanahan, 2006). The panel found that the same five components identified by the National Reading Panel and required by Reading First are also important for ELLs, but that there are several ways to adjust instruction that can be beneficial for ELLs. In other words, one size does not fit all. As we already noted, our purpose in this chapter is *not* to illustrate how to teach reading to ELLs (for practical suggestions for teaching reading to ELLs, see Frances, Rivera, Lesaux, Kieffer, & Rivera, 2006). Instead, our goal is to point out key differences in instruction in each of these areas, with a focus on those aspects of instruction that can be particularly challenging for ELLs and can lead to false impressions about why they are struggling. It is these problematic areas that can confuse teachers and contribute to the over-referral of culturally and linguistically diverse students to special education. We summarize these principles in Table 4.1 and also describe them.

Phonological Awareness

Phonological awareness is the ability to identify and manipulate the parts of spoken language. Phonemic awareness is a subcategory of phonological awareness, and is the ability to identify and manipulate the phonemes or sounds in spoken words. Numerous research studies indicate that phonological awareness is predictive of later reading ability (National Reading Panel, 2000). With ELLs, phonological awareness in English or Spanish seems to predict English reading achievement (Chiappe, Siegel, & Gottardo, 2002; Lindsey, Manis, & Bailey, 2003). In fact, Spanish

Table 4.1   Possible Problematic Aspects of Instruction for ELLs in the "Five Big Ideas" of Reading

Reading Component	Potential Challenges for ELLs

Phonological Awareness	• When the student's first language, or L1, does not include some English phonemes:
	  o The student is not accustomed to hearing these sounds.
	  o It can be quite difficult to distinguish between sounds.
	  o Pronouncing new sounds can be difficult.
	  o Phonological tasks in general become more challenging.

Alphabetic Principle	• Some orthographies are very different than English; even when the orthography of the student's L1 is similar to English, such as with Spanish, differences can be quite confusing:
	  o Letters might look the same but represent different sounds.
	  o Unfamiliar English sounds and their various spellings can make decoding and spelling difficult.
	  o Not knowing the meanings of words limits the ELL reader's ability to use context clues.
	  o Learning letters and sounds can seem very abstract.

Fluency	• ELLs typically have fewer opportunities to read aloud in English and receive feedback than their English speaking peers. • ELLs may read more slowly, with less understanding. • ELLs can have an accent and still read fluently.

Vocabulary	• Students may become good word callers but not understand what they are reading.
	• ELLs can be confused by common words, such as
	  o prepositions (e.g., "on," "above")
	  o pronouns (e.g., "she," "they")
	  o cohesion markers (e.g., "therefore," "however")
	  o words with multiple meanings (e.g., "bat," "light")
	  o figurative language such as similes (e.g., "swims like a fish") or metaphors (e.g., "his stomach was a bottomless pit")
	  o idioms (e.g., "to know something inside out")
	• False cognates can perplex students (e.g., "fast" in German means "almost"; "embarasada" in Spanish means "pregnant").

Reading Comprehension	• Many factors affect comprehension, such as
	  o oral language proficiency
	  o word recognition skills
	  o fluency
	  o vocabulary knowledge

Reading Component	Potential Challenges for ELLs
	○ the ability to use comprehension strategies ○ variations in text structure ○ interest ○ cultural differences • To determine what students comprehend, teachers should ○ provide them with alternative ways to show understanding (e.g., in their native language, using diagrams) ○ focus more on content than grammatical errors or accents

phonological awareness might be a better predictor of English word reading than English or Spanish oral proficiency or English word recognition (Durgunoglu, Nagy, & Hancin-Bhatt, 1993).

For ELLs learning to read in English, phonological awareness can be especially challenging when the student's native language does not include some English phonemes (Antunez, 2002). For example, most dialects in Spanish do not include "sh" or the short vowel sound for "i." When this happens, the student is not accustomed to hearing these sounds and it can be quite difficult to distinguish them from other sounds. Pronouncing the new sounds can also be tricky for the student. Phonological tasks in general become more challenging. If teachers are not aware of these challenges, they might assume that the child has a deficit in auditory discrimination and/or in phonological awareness. Weak auditory discrimination and phonological awareness can be early signs of a learning disability, thus the potential for misunderstanding is great. What teachers need to remember is that confusion about sounds is a natural by-product of learning a second language. Teachers can help ELLs with phonological awareness by finding out which phonemes do not exist in the student's native language and helping the student discriminate the sounds. Teachers can also help by not prematurely drawing the conclusion that the student has a disability.

Alphabetic Principle

The alphabetic principle is the understanding of sound-symbol correspondence, or, in other words, which letters make which sounds. It also involves combining sounds into words. For ELLs, learning the alphabetic principle in English can be challenging if they have not already developed this literacy skill in their first language and/or have not acquired sufficient oral English proficiency to make sense of the words they are reading. The process can be quite abstract and meaningless for them. Many ELLs become good word-callers—that is, they become good at sounding out words without knowing their meaning (August & Shanahan, 2006). In fact, they sometimes do better than their English-only peers on subtests requiring students to read nonsense words. After all, most everything they are reading seems like nonsense to them anyway.

When students are already literate in their first language, learning to read in English is easier. This is particularly true when the orthographic systems of the two languages are similar, as with Spanish or French, and much more challenging when they are not, as with Chinese or Korean. Yet, even when the orthographies have much in common, as with English and Spanish, differences can be quite confusing. For example, the sounds represented by the letters *b, c, d, f, 1, m, n, p, q, s,* and *t* are alike enough that they transfer to English (Antunez, 2002). Vowels, however, look the same in Spanish and English but represent different sounds. Thus, when a child pronounces a vowel sound as he would in Spanish, the word sounds incorrect (e.g., saying "beet" instead of "bit"). Unfamiliar English sounds and their various spellings can make decoding as well as spelling difficult. Another challenge is that not knowing the meanings of words limits the ELL reader's ability to use context clues to help her figure out how to read words (August & Shanahan, 2006).

It is easier for us to learn and remember new information we can plug in or connect to existing schema. "Schema" refers to the way our brains organize and store concepts we already know. For example, try this exercise as a test of this idea: Have someone name ten random words that have no apparent connection to one another. See how many you can remember. Then ask the person to name ten words that are clearly related, such as different rooms in a house. Again, try to remember them. Which task was easier? Which way did you remember more words? Most likely you remembered more words the second way because it is easier to remember information we can readily connect. If you were trying to remember rooms in a house, most likely you visualized a house, and perhaps even pictured yourself walking through different rooms.

What does this have to do with ELLs learning phonics? Often students are asked to learn sounds in quite abstract ways, perhaps quite unintentionally. For example, Zoo-phonics is a common way to teach letter names and sounds to kindergartners by well-meaning teachers who assume they are helping students connect with their prior knowledge. Yet, "Queenie Quail," "Umber Umbrella Bird," and "Nigel Nightowl" can seem quite meaningless to children who have not been exposed to these names or animals prior to starting school. ELLs are not only being asked to learn new letter names and sounds, but also to acquire new concepts and vocabulary.

If the teacher does not help students make these connections and allow them more time for this additional learning, what might she assume when they struggle? Many teachers erroneously conclude that their ELLs must have LD or "can't learn to read" (Orosco, 2007). ELLs benefit from explicit instruction that is comprehensible and at their level (August & Shanahan, 2006).

Fluency

Fluency is the ability to read quickly and accurately, with expression. Fluency requires both word recognition and comprehension. One challenge ELLs face is that they typically are afforded fewer opportunities to read aloud in English and receive feedback than their English speaking peers (August & Shanahan, 2007). It is not uncommon for them to read more slowly than their fluent English classmates, and with less understanding. One way to help build fluency is to make sure students understand text and can decode all words before they read it. Opportunities to hear a more expert reader model fluent, expressive reading help, such as through echo reading or partner reading. Struggling ELL readers might also listen to and follow along with books on tape or on CD (Hiebert et al., 1998; Peregoy & Boyle, 2001). Antunez (2002) reminds us that fluency should not be confused with having an accent. Many ELLs and fully proficient English as a second language speakers read English with an accent, but they can still read fluently. When ELLs read more slowly and lack expression, teachers should recognize that this is quite common for ELLs and does not indicate a learning disability. At the same time, teachers should provide them with additional opportunities to practice oral reading.

Vocabulary

ELLs by definition are in the process of acquiring English and do not have English vocabularies as extensive as those of their fully English proficient peers. They might, however, have extensive vocabularies in their native language. How to assist ELLs increase their vocabularies is one of the greatest challenges their teachers face (Antunez, 2002). Vocabulary development is of critical importance, especially considering that vocabulary knowledge affects fluency as well as comprehension (Beck, McKeown, & Kucan, 2002). It is not uncommon for ELLs to be able to decode words without understanding what they mean (i.e., word calling). Many teachers understand that their students benefit from explicit instruction and the preteaching of key vocabulary terms they will encounter in text (e.g., content vocabulary in science, such as "ecosystem" or "photosynthesis"). Yet they might not consider that their ELLs also need help with more common words that can be confusing, such as prepositions (e.g., "on," "in," "above"), pronouns (e.g., such as "she" in the sentences, "Maria was not feeling well. She hoped she would be able to leave early."), and cohesion markers (e.g., "therefore," "however"). Words with multiple meanings (e.g., "bat," "light"), figurative language such as similes (e.g., "as quick as a cricket," "swims like a fish") or metaphors (e.g., "his stomach was a bottomless pit"), and idioms (e.g., "a piece of cake," "to know something inside out") can be especially challenging for ELLs.

Many words in English have cognates in other languages (i.e., words that are the same or similar, such as "bandage," which is the same in French and English, or "animal," which is the same in Spanish and English). Knowing this can be quite helpful for ELLs who are already literate in their first language, especially when the teacher points them out. Yet, false cognates can be quite confusing for students (e.g., "fast" in German means "almost" rather than "rapid"; "embarasada" in Spanish means "pregnant").

Teachers need to keep in mind that there is a difference between words for which the student understands the underlying concept and knows the word in her native language, and words for which the meaning is unknown in both the student's first language as well as in English (August & Shanahan, 2006). When the student already understands the concept behind a new word in English, simply providing the native language label most likely will facilitate understanding. Yet when the concept is a new one, the teacher should provide more extensive instruction in what the concept means. In any case, the teacher should not assume that ELL students' understandings of words are the same as those of their fully English proficient peers.

Just because students are in the process of developing their English vocabularies, this does not mean they might have LD or lack intelligence. As a group, ELLs are every bit as intelligent as their fully English proficient peers. Yet it seems to be human nature to assume otherwise. Astute teachers are aware of this and make sure they do all they can to help their students develop their vocabularies, while at the same time being careful not to judge their students as somehow less capable.

Reading Comprehension

Reading comprehension is the ultimate goal of reading (Snow, 2002). After all, knowing how to decode words has little value if comprehension is missing. Reading comprehension is a complex process of constructing meaning by coordinating a number of processes, including decoding, word reading, and fluency along with the integration of background knowledge and previous experiences (Snow, 2002). Many factors can influence the reading comprehension of ELLs, such as oral language proficiency, word recognition skills, fluency, vocabulary knowledge, interest, and the ability to use comprehension strategies. Variations in text structure (i.e., the way narrative and expository texts are organized) can be perplexing for ELLs and affect their comprehension. Dissimilarities in cultural understandings also make a difference (August & Shanahan, 2006). For example, the typical wedding ceremony is quite different across cultures. Thus, a student who is reading about a wedding in the United States but whose background knowledge is about weddings in India will have different expectations for what will happen in the text, and may become confused.

There are many promising practices teachers can use to help ELLs understand what they read and develop their reading comprehension skills (August & Shanahan, 2007); however, these techniques are not the focus of this chapter. Teachers typically spend little time actually teaching reading comprehension strategies to their students (Durkin, 1977/1978; Klingner et al., 2007). Rather, they are more likely to ask students comprehension questions about text they have listened to or read. Even though only a few students may raise their hands to answer (and probably not the ELLs), the teacher is likely to call on a student to respond, evaluate the student's response, and then move on (Cazden, 2001). The teacher might assume students understand better than they do, and then later wonder why they did not do well on the test designed to assess their learning of the material. Or, teachers might think that their ELLs understand very little when in fact they comprehend a fair amount. ELLs may understand more than they can demonstrate orally or in writing in English. If they are allowed to show what they have learned using their native language or with alternatives to oral or written responses, such as through diagrams or demonstrations, oftentimes it becomes clear that they comprehend much more than was at first apparent. Teachers might also draw the wrong conclusions about ELLs' comprehension if they pay more attention to students' grammatical errors, their accents when speaking, or the mechanics of their writing, than they do to the substance of their responses. When the goal is to determine the extent to which students understand the material they are learning, the teacher's focus should be on the content rather than the form of students' answers.

Two More "Big Ideas"

In addition to the five big ideas discussed above, the National Literacy Panel on Language Minority Children and Youth (2006) noted that oral language development should be considered an essential component of effective instruction for ELLs. Motivation is another factor that is critical for all students, and perhaps especially important for culturally and linguistically diverse students who are more likely to underachieve in schools across the United States (Lee, 2002). We describe these next.

ORAL LANGUAGE

For ELLs, the challenge is not just how to provide explicit instruction in reading and writing, but also how to develop oral English proficiency. Oral language proficiency affects literacy acquisition (August & Shanahan, 2006). When students' oral language improves, so do their reading fluency and comprehension. Generic literacy programs are inadequate for ELLs because they guide teachers to explicitly teach only reading and writing skills, assuming that the prerequisite oral language skills are sufficiently under control (Gentile, 2004). Such programs neglect much needed explicit teaching for oral language development. To more successfully facilitate literacy acquisition of ELLs, Gentile recommends that literacy programs emphasize explicit teaching of both talk and text. "Oracy" is Gentile's term for literacy instruction that includes explicit teaching for literacy and oral language acquisition, as well as a focus on the child's culture and an emphasis on the importance of child-teacher interactions, as represented by Figure 4.1.

The less than full English oral proficiency of students who are becoming bilingual plays out in different ways. As already discussed, students may be unfamiliar with key vocabulary words. They likely are confused by English grammatical structures. They may need to strengthen their narration and retelling skills. They might not respond well to large group instruction, or refrain from contributing during whole class activities. They may have little understanding of the connections between oral and written language (Gentile, 2004).

It is important for teachers not to assume their ELLs have sufficient oral language proficiency to benefit from instruction. Harry and Klingner (2006) observed literacy instruction in classrooms with ELLs at beginning levels of English proficiency and noted that some teachers almost exclusively provided verbal explanations without the visual cues or other scaffolding that might have helped their instruction be more comprehensible to students. It was obvious to the observers that many students did not understand, yet teachers were likely to scold students for "not listening"

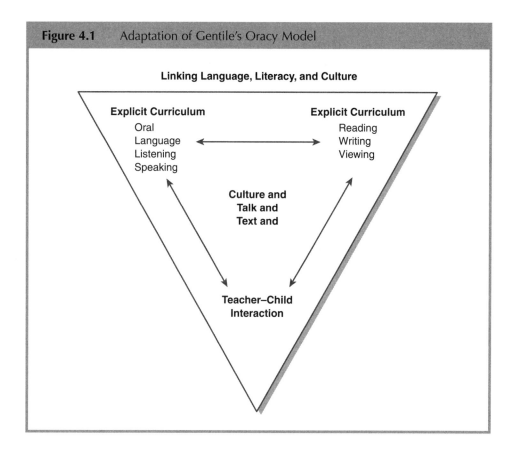

Figure 4.1   Adaptation of Gentile's Oracy Model

or "not paying attention." One such teacher referred several of her students to the school's Child Study Team (i.e., special education preferral team) because she suspected they had LD, mental retardation, or an emotional/behavioral disorder.

Teachers should observe their struggling learners closely to determine what their oral language needs might be. Frances et al. (2006) emphasize that "more structured 'talk' in classrooms across the United States would provide increased opportunities to informally assess students' oral language development in different contexts and for students to monitor and become more aware of, and active in, their own language development" (p. 28). A period of daily oracy instruction would be a logical, appropriate prereferral intervention for emergent readers struggling with literacy and language acquisition. In her research with ELLs, Haager (2004) found that those teachers who emphasized oral academic language development achieved greater gains in their students' reading scores than teachers who did not (see the Research to Practice box on the following page).

Research on Reading Achievement for English Language Learners

Haager and colleagues (2004) examined the critical features of beginning reading instruction that lead to improved reading achievement among English language learners receiving instruction in English. Their research studies took place in urban schools with high percentages of ELLs. The researchers observed reading instruction to determine which aspects of first grade literacy instruction were seen most often in classrooms with higher academic outcomes for ELLs. They conducted pre- and post-testing of students in key areas of beginning reading instruction and compared these test scores with their ratings of teachers in several domains on an observation instrument.

Haager and colleagues (2004) found that it is very important to integrate English language development with basic reading instruction. Effective teachers integrated vocabulary and language development into their core reading instruction when teaching ELLs (e.g., teacher-planned specific vocabulary-building activities). Furthermore, Haager suggests that during reading intervention, instruction should integrate English language development and reinforce vocabulary taught in the core reading lessons. Haager (2004) indicates that in order to make significant reading gains with ELLs, teachers need to

1. Use effective instructional techniques in general

2. Adjust their instruction for individuals having difficulty

3. Engage their students in interactive and engaging oral language, vocabulary, and comprehension development

4. Provide high-quality explicit instruction in phonemic awareness and decoding

MOTIVATION

There is no doubt that the extent to which students are motivated affects their learning. Snow, Burns, and Griffin (1998) stressed the significance of motivation in the precursor to the National Reading Panel report (2000), "Preventing Reading Difficulties in Young Children." They wrote that "motivation is crucial" (p. 3 of Executive Summary) and noted that one of the principle reasons students struggle to learn to read is a loss of motivation. Frustration can lead to a lack of motivation, as can tasks that seem meaningless or disconnected from the realities of everyday life. Certainly many ELLs are faced with learning situations like this on a daily basis. Rueda, MacGillivray, Monzó, and Arzubiaga (2001) emphasized the role of context and sociocultural factors in influencing reading engagement and motivation for ELLs. They noted that motivation is not only something the student brings to the learning situation, but also is an aspect of the task and is a part of the learning environment. When ELLs seem to lack motivation, before teachers conclude that they do not want to learn, are lazy, or do not care, they should first look at factors such as whether the assignment is meaningful, relevant, and at an appropriate instructional level, and whether the students understand what is being asked of them and have all of the tools they need to accomplish the task.

What does a motivating program look like? Careful thought is given to the nature of the texts and activities used for instructing ELLs. The texts should be both interesting and at an appropriate level to nourish children's developing literacy and language skills. The topics, the relevancy, and the language all affect how children interact with the texts and how well they learn from them. Students bring linguistic and cultural resources to school that can be used to construct a relevant and engaging curriculum. Reading, writing, listening, and speaking should build upon these "funds of knowledge" (Moll & Greenberg, 1990). Instruction should account for the impact of culture and experience on cognition, literacy learning, behavior, oral language development, and motivation. We offer a synopsis of the Early Author's Program (Bernhard et al., 2006) as an example of a successful research-based literacy program that capitalizes on students' strengths and interests.

Research to Practice

The Early Authors Program (EAP)

The Early Authors Program is a language intervention program for bilingual preschoolers with the main goal of promoting early bilingual literacy. The program combines "effective teaching, appropriate recognition of the value of home language maintenance, and strong support for both cognitive engagement and personal identity investment in the learning process" (Bernhard et al., 2004). It was first implemented in Miami-Dade County, Florida, with 1,179 children of families receiving subsidized daycare in 32 early childhood centers. Children participated in bilingual literacy activities that involved writing and illustrating their own dual-language books in which the children themselves were the protagonists. They produced 3,286 books. Essential features of the program include

- home-school joint productive activities
- bilingual literacy activities involving children and their families writing and illustrating dual language books with children as the protagonists (authoring, reading, storytelling)

(Continued)

(Continued)

- children taught to recite culturally relevant rhymes and poems in their home languages
- high value placed on home language maintenance and English acquisition
- cognitive engagement and identity investment in the learning process
- professional development for teachers including on-site coaching of teachers by literacy specialists
- teachers taught to relate letter teaching to names of children, their friends, and family members
- monthly workshops for parents
- bookmaking materials provided (i.e., computers, digital cameras, color printers, laminators)

In their investigation of the effectiveness of EAP, Bernhardt et al. (2006) found that EAP children gained in language and cognitive skills, as measured by standardized instruments. The three- and four-year-old EAP children's gain in language development (both expressive and receptive) was about ten months compared to the control children's gain of about three months. In other words, participation in the EAP intervention prevented the children from continuing to fall farther behind their national peers. Also, the affective and cognitive engagement of the children was markedly high. The book writing work was social and interactive and the affective climate was warm and intimate. The work was personally meaningful and relevant to the children and their families, thus affirming the children's identities. Indeed, the EAP researchers noted that the EAP children developed an "affective bond to literacy" (Bernhard et al., 2005, p. 31). They emphasized that affect matters; in other words, learning is influenced by emotion (Wolfe & Brandt, 1998).

EAP also had a positive effect on the literacy environment of the classrooms. The number of literacy-related activities in which the teachers engaged increased significantly. Teachers liked the EAP program and believed it was sustainable. They reported positive effects on children's identity and self-esteem and that the project was a success for all involved: the children, their parents, and the teachers themselves.

DECISION POINTS WHEN STUDENTS STRUGGLE WITH READING

What should teachers do when their ELLs are struggling? What if some students really do have LD? How can teachers tell which students should receive additional interventions or who to refer for an evaluation for possible placement in special education? A useful rule of thumb is to look at how many ELLs are struggling. If the majority of ELLs are making little progress, the teacher should focus on improving instruction. If most ELLs are doing well and only a few are struggling, the teacher should look more closely at what is going on with those individual students and consider that they may need additional support.

First let us focus on classrooms where the majority of ELLs are struggling. How should classroom teachers adjust instruction when their ELLs are making little progress? Effective teachers of ELLs must become keen observers of children and should have a wide repertoire of instructional practices at their fingertips in order to match instruction to a particular child's needs. Instructional approaches that demand one particular pathway are inappropriate for ELLs because they lack the flexibility needed to meet the widely varying needs of the ELL population. This is problematic because when reading instruction is scripted or a method insists on a predetermined sequence of what is to be learned and how it is to be learned, the responsibility to adjust falls on the *child* to match the curriculum. The child who cannot meet the program where it begins and stay in step soon falls behind. In such programs, teachers have little flexibility to adapt the program to meet children's individual differences. Thus, the first question the teacher should ask when ELLs are struggling is

1. Is my instruction culturally, linguistically, and pedagogically appropriate to meet students' needs?
   If the answer appears to be "no," then the next question should be

2. How can I adjust instruction to be more appropriate?

This is true whether the teacher is in a school implementing the Response to Intervention Model (see Chapter 3), or in a school using a more traditional model.

Optimal literacy instruction for ELLs accounts for the influence of culture and experience on cognition and learning, behavior and communication, language development and motivation. Some LD diagnoses of ELLs are made not because the students have internal deficits of some kind, but rather because they have not received an adequate opportunity to learn (Harry & Klingner, 2006). Another way to think about this is not that the children have disabilities, but that they are in "disabling contexts." Many ELLs are provided with too few and insufficient opportunities to develop their language and literacy skills. Prior to referring a young ELL for evaluation of a reading disability or for more intensive interventions as part of a RTI model, teachers should consider the types of language and literacy instruction to which the child has had access. The following questions may guide teachers as they reflect on their instructional practices for language and literacy learning for ELLs:

1. Have I developed a strong, positive relationship with the child and his or her family?

2. Do I personalize instruction? Do I value the child's linguistic and cultural background? Do I connect classroom learning to the child's daily experiences?

3. Do I give enough attention to affect, interest, and motivation?

4. Do I pay sufficient attention to the development of oral language?

5. Am I aware of aspects of reading that can be confusing for ELLs?

6. Have I found out which sounds and letters are different in the child's first language than English so that I can clarify misunderstandings and provide additional practice?

7. Do I adjust instruction to provide students with additional support when they do not seem to understand (e.g., explicit instruction at their level, more opportunities for meaningful practice)?

8. Are the books I use at levels students can read and understand?

9. Do I preteach key vocabulary and use multimedia, real items, appealing photos, charts, and other visuals to help make instruction comprehensible?

10. Do I focus more on the content of students' responses than the form when checking for comprehension, and provide multiple and varied ways of demonstrating learning?

When the answer to most of these questions is "yes" and most ELLs in the class are progressing, yet a few continue to struggle, additional support should be provided to those students. Researchers now suggest examining both students' rate of progress in comparison with that of similar peers and also whether students are reaching learning goals, or benchmarks (Compton, Fuchs, Fuchs, & Bryant, 2006; also, see Chapter 3 on the RTI Model). Struggling ELLs should be provided with small group language and literacy interventions that are explicit, responsive to their needs, personalized, relevant, and not based on deficit views of the students.

CONCLUSION AND A CAVEAT

The point of this chapter has been to help teachers understand the struggles faced by their ELLs while learning to read so that they do not misjudge them and inappropriately refer them to special education. However, we must offer a caveat. Some ELLs truly do have LD and would benefit from the extra support they would receive in special education. We do not want our advice to be construed as suggesting teachers should wait until ELLs are fully proficient in English before considering whether they might have LD.

In some schools, the tendency has been to take a "wait and see" approach and delay addressing the possibility that ELLs are experiencing reading difficulties due to language or learning disabilities (Frances et al., 2006). Because the characteristics associated with language acquisition can mirror those of LD, school personnel have wanted to avoid the possibility of incorrectly placing a child in special education. Certainly we share the concerns behind this approach; however, just as it is a problem to identify a child as having a disability who does not, it is also a problem to hold off on providing interventions to ELLs who really need them. For this reason, we suggest following the guidelines outlined in this chapter so that reading instruction for all ELLs improves and fewer inappropriate referrals are made. Once we have done that, we can feel more confident that the few students who are still experiencing difficulties will benefit from explicit, intensive interventions above and beyond what they are receiving in their general education classrooms.

5 Data-Driven Decision Making in a Multi-Tiered Model

John J. Hoover

As previously discussed in Chapter 3, the education of students who struggle with learning is currently involved in a significant movement away from the more traditional "wait to fail" model (i.e., prereferral, referral, assessment, placement) to one of early intervening as soon as potential learning or behavior problems are observed. The emphasis in today's schools is on providing layers or tiers of interventions based on how well a learner responds to instruction. While not a new concept, multi-tiered instruction is in the process of being implemented in virtually every state and the District of Columbia (Hoover, Baca, Love, & Seanz, in review). One of the purported strengths of a multi-tiered model of instruction is early identification of the needs of struggling learners. However, educators must ensure that problems experienced over the past decades associated with misinterpreting learning differences, or language acquisition, as disabilities are avoided as they implement multi-tiered instruction. This chapter describes the data that educators should collect and factors they should consider when making decisions about why a child might be struggling. The focus of the chapter is on what to do initially and during the early stages of providing interventions to a child who does not seem to be progressing.

Within a multi-tiered model is the process of identifying effective interventions and determining progress toward established curricular benchmarks using data generated through ongoing progress monitoring

(Brown-Chidsey & Steege, 2005). Therefore, as students begin to show signs of struggling with learning, the process to be followed includes

1. Determining whether initial efforts included the proper implementation and use of evidence-based practices

2. Determining of needed supplemental support to complement the general class curriculum

3. Selecting appropriate supplemental evidence-based intervention

4. Implementing selected intervention

5. Gathering data to determine effectiveness of the intervention in meeting student needs

While all of these components in the multi-tiered/RTI process are important, once a learner has been identified as struggling and supplemental instruction has been implemented, the documentation using quantifiable data becomes essential for making informed decisions.

DATA-DRIVEN DECISION MAKING

The foundation for making effective decisions for struggling learners throughout the multi-tier process is found in the evidence or data that illustrate level of progress. As struggling learners are provided supplemental interventions and ongoing progress monitoring occurs, educators are collecting, charting, and analyzing data. For example, the specific number of times a learner uses a skill or the number of words read correctly within a two-minute timeframe would be counted and charted by the teacher. This progress monitoring may continue for two school weeks and at that time the problem-solving team would review the learner's progress using the charted or graphed data points (i.e., number of correct words used). As a result, the team would be using the quantified data to form decisions concerning the effectiveness of the evidence-based intervention selected (i.e., data-driven decision making). While educators have used assessment data for years to determine the progress of struggling learners through prereferral interventions, the progress monitoring and data decision making found within multi-tiered instruction is more frequent and rigorous. In effect, some of the practices and procedures already in our schools through prereferral are consistent with and support multi-tiered instruction in the hopes of further advancing the education for all struggling learners, including ELLs.

MULTI-TIERED INSTRUCTION AND PREREFERRAL INTERVENTIONS

For several decades, school systems have followed a prereferral intervention process for selecting and implementing interventions to meet the needs of struggling learners in the classroom. However, a more extended period of time elapsed prior to beginning prereferral interventions, and the documentation of the effectiveness of prereferral interventions was less formal than proposed by multi-tiered instructional models. Therefore, as we move into the widespread implementation of multi-tiered models, we should build on the strengths of what we have learned from the prereferral process while simultaneously avoiding similar mistakes, particularly as they relate to the use of data to make educational decisions for struggling English language learners.

When considering the use of data for making informed decision, for ELLs, of particular concern is the extent to which the cultural and linguistic needs of struggling learners are incorporated into multi-tiered education. Therefore, many of the same issues that have confronted prereferral teams over the years continue to challenge multi-tiered instructional teams as the needs of struggling learners are more quickly identified and addressed.

Specifically, the types of documents and information used to base instructional decisions, noncompliance with various state and district laws or guidelines, as well as an indifference to using valid and appropriate information to make informed educational data-based decisions for ELLs (Figueroa & Newsome, 2004; Klingner & Harry, 2004; Wilkinson, Ortiz & Robertson-Courtney, 2004) must be addressed if ELLs are to be effectively educated in today's instructional multi-tiered environments. Several elements associated with the existing prereferral process are also included in a multi-tiered model. However, we must ensure that similar problems, or barriers to effective education, often resulting from the prereferral process be avoided through the multi-tiered process. In order for a multi-tiered model to build upon the successes, and avoid making similar mistakes, of existing prereferral intervention models the following, at minimum, must occur:

- Educators must be properly trained to select and implement evidence-based interventions.
- Educators require support to properly implement evidence-based interventions.
- Multi-tier teams must include representation from all appropriate educators (e.g., ELL teachers, special educator, general class teacher).
- Selected evidence-based practices must have research to support their use with the target population of students (e.g., second language learners).

- Progress monitoring strategies and instruments must be clearly understood by the teacher.
- Data related to student progress must, in part, be quantified, charted, and used as a foundation for making subsequent educational decisions.

As suggested, the use of data-driven decisions is fundamental to the successful implementation of multi-tiered instruction and RTI. In order for this to occur for ELLs, several educational factors or issues must be addressed by problem-solving teams. These are discussed below.

CLARIFYING EDUCATIONAL ISSUES IN THE DECISION MAKING FOR ENGLISH LANGUAGE LEARNERS STRUGGLING IN LEARNING

Screening is the first formal step in the overall assessment and progress-monitoring process for identifying struggling students. As previously discussed in Chapter 3, multi- or three-tiered instruction is based on progress monitoring data reflecting student progress toward curricular benchmarks when being taught with evidence-based interventions. In addition to progress-monitoring test data, other relevant information about the learner is important to adequately provide the proper level and intensity of interventions to struggling ELLs.

When implemented properly, the multi-tiered process could be of significant benefit to ELLs as more formal and in-depth screening is undertaken to determine whether cultural or linguistic factors contribute to suspected learning or behavioral problems. Along with this, a major issue for ELLs is to ensure that the influence of language or cultural factors on suspected learning and behavioral problems is clarified and understood by all involved in the multi-tiered instructional process. One of the more effective ways to ensure appropriate interpretation of struggling learner needs, and reduce bias when working with ELLs, is to be knowledgeable of behaviors that may be more reflective of typical behaviors associated with the student's cultural and linguistic background, rather than as misinterpreted learning/behavior disorders. Table 5.1 provides an overview of selected behaviors often associated with disabilities as well as those typical of second language acquisition and associated cultural values and norms. As shown, some of the same behaviors reflect each of these three aspects, and when considering the severity of needs for ELLs struggling in learning, behaviors must be put into a proper cultural/linguistic context to avoid misinterpreting difference as disability.

Table 5.1   Similarities Among Cultural/Linguistic Behaviors and Suspected Learning
Disabilities (LD)

Learning/Behavior Challenges Often Associated With LD	Expected Behaviors in Stages When Learning a Second Language (English-L2)	Cultural Behaviors or Values
Preschool Children	**The Silent Period Stage**	**Cultural Characteristics**
Language • Slow speech development • Pronunciation problems • Difficulty learning new words • Difficulty following simple directions • Difficulty understanding questions • Difficulty expressing needs • Difficulty rhyming words	• Difficulty following directions • Speaks very little English • May be silent, not respond when spoken to • Difficulty understanding questions • Difficulty expressing needs • May be withdrawn/ show low self-esteem • May seem to exhibit poor attention and concentration • Pronunciation problems	• May view time differently (e.g., starting times, deadlines) • Anxiety, stress due to process of adapting to new cultural environment • Acting out may reflect lack of experience with formal schooling • Differences in preferred style of learning may reflect cultural norms • External locus of control may be emphasized in some cultures • Time management abilities reflect cultural values toward time
Cognition • Trouble memorizing • Difficulty with cause and effect • Difficulty with basic concepts	**The Early Production Stage** • May be withdrawn • Speaks in single words and phrases • May seem to have trouble concentrating • Phrases may contain notable grammatical errors • May be easily frustrated	• Independent work may be discouraged, in favor of group work/ collaboration • Coping strategies may vary by culture
Attention • High distractibility • Impulsive behavior • Unusually restless • Difficulty staying on task • Difficulty changing activities	**The Intermediate Stage** • Learner is approaching age appropriate levels • Still makes errors in speech, reading, and writing in English (academic, behavioral, cultural, social)	• Confusion with time and space may be due to lack of familiarity with new cultural expectations • Behaviors involving touch, movement, proximity to others may vary
Social • Trouble interacting with others • Easily frustrated		• Kinesthetic strategies may receive greater emphasis

(Continued)

Table 5.1 (Continued)

Learning/Behavior Problems Often Associated With LD	Expected Behaviors in Stages When Learning a Second Language (English-L2)	Cultural Behaviors or Values
Preschool Children *Social* • Withdrawn • Poor self-control **Elementary School-Aged** *Language* • Slow learning sound-symbol correspondence • Difficulty remembering sight words • Difficulty retelling a story in sequence *Attention* • Difficulty concentrating • Difficulty following multiple directions • Difficulty finishing work on time • Difficulty following multiple directions *Social* • Difficulty interpreting facial expressions • Difficulty understanding social situations • Apparent lack of common sense • Misinterpreting behavior of peers	**The Intermediate Stage** • May seem more proficient than she is • May seem slow processing challenging language • May be confused by idioms, slang conveyed in English • May understand more than he is able to demonstrate • May seem to have poor auditory memory	• Ways of showing respect may vary (e.g., lowered eyes vs. eye contact) • Discourse styles may vary (e.g., overlapping talk vs. waiting one's turn) • Offering a different opinion may be considered a sign of disrespect • Gender differences may influence the extent to which girls speak • May not be used to learning through question-answer exchanges (e.g., preferring observation)

Source: Adapted from Berger (2000); Baca & Cervantes (2004); Collier & Hoover (1987); Cummins (1984); Hoover & Collier (1985); Jerrell (2000); Ortiz & Wilkinson (1990).

In addition, over the past three decades, many researchers have discussed alternative possible explanations for an ELL's behaviors within the context of their cultural and linguistic backgrounds, rather than learning or behavior disorders (Adler, 1975; Baca & Cervantes, 2004; Collier, 1988;

Collier & Hoover, 1987b; Donovan & Cross, 2002; Figueroa & Newsome, 2004; Grossman, 1995; Hoover & Collier, 2003; Klingner & Harry, 2004; Lachat, 2004; Loe & Miranda, 2002; Nazzrro, 1981; Wilkinson, Ortiz, & Robertson-Courtney, 2004). Discussions in these and other sources emphasize the notion that educators must consider any suspected learning or behavior problem relative to the struggling student's cultural and linguistic values, norms, and expectations—especially when using these behaviors as a basis for making multi-tiered instructional decisions. To assist the reader, Table 5.2, developed from information found in the above sources, provides more specific examples of possible cultural or linguistic explanations for several behaviors that may be associated with struggling learners. These are not all-inclusive and may not apply to all ELLs; however, in order to effectively and appropriately educate an ELL in multi-tiered instruction, alternative explanations based on cultural and linguistic background must be explored.

As shown, a variety of plausible explanations may account for ELLs' behaviors as they attempt to learn a second language and/or adjust to a new cultural environment (i.e., acculturation). These should be considered to reduce biased decision making in multi-tiered instruction. Educators teaching struggling ELLs must make every effort to determine if exhibited behaviors are typical and expected due to various cultural and linguistic situations and select appropriate evidence-based interventions accordingly.

Determining Difference Versus Disability

As discussed, during the implementation of multi-tiered interventions for ELLs, one of the more fundamental issues confronting educators in the decision making process is determining whether an area of need is due to

1. A learning disability

2. A learning difference resulting from culturally and linguistically diverse factors (examples provided in Tables 5.1 and 5.2)

3. A combination of the above two

The unique ways that individuals successfully acquire, process, integrate, and utilize knowledge and skills (which may deviate from what is typically accepted or preferred in schools or individual classrooms) reflect a learning *difference.* Conversely, a learning *disability* or *disorder* is represented by a condition within the learner, which interferes with or limits the individual's ability to successfully acquire, process, integrate, and generalize knowledge and skills (Hoover, Klingner, Baca, & Patton, 2008). Members of teams who receive, review, and act upon progress monitoring data should bear in mind that a primary difference between a learning

Table 5.2 Cultural and Linguistic Explanations for ELLs Who Struggle in Learning

Exhibited Behaviors	Plausible Cultural/Linguistic Explanations
Extended periods of silence	May be associated with limited English proficiency level and/or level of acculturation (i.e., process of adapting to new environment such as a new school or classroom); some cultures encourage children to be quiet as a sign of respect
Confusion with locus of control	Some cultures teach that events are out of the control of individuals (i.e., external locus of control) and this should not be misinterpreted as not caring or requiring intervention
Indifference to time	The concept of time is often perceived differently in various cultures and may be significantly different than time emphasized in U.S. schools (e.g., completion of tasks or the making of important decisions are more frequently based on when the individual[s] perceive that the time is right rather than on a specific time indicated by a clock)
Social withdrawal	Shy behavior may be associated with the process of adjusting or acculturating to a new environment (e.g., U.S. schools/classrooms) and/or with learning English as second language
Acting out/aggressive behavior	Some cultures may teach that assertive behavior (e.g., standing up for oneself) is desirable social behavior; inexperience with U.S. classroom rules may also account for acting out behaviors
Difficulty with independent work	Some cultures may value group performance over individual achievement and thus students may be unfamiliar with independent, competitive learning and prefer cooperative group learning
Perceived lack of significance of school achievement	While education is highly valued across cultures, sometimes other priorities in that culture may take priority (e.g., family needs; spring harvest)
Poor performance on tests taken in English	Tests in English become an English test for limited English proficient students; test results in English must be interpreted relative to the learner's English proficiency level
Low self-esteem	Students from different cultures or linguistic backgrounds may initially experience difficulty while adjusting to new cultural expectations and learning a new language, temporarily negatively impacting a child's self concept
Differences in perception of everyday items	Different cultures may view everyday concepts differently than the mainstream culture (e.g., personal space, sharing of belongings, gender, meaning of color, directions) and knowledge of how cultures view these and related items is necessary to make informed decisions

Exhibited Behaviors	Plausible Cultural/Linguistic Explanations
Increased anxiety	Stress associated with adjusting to a new culture and/or learning a new language often results in increased anxiety in learners until they feel more comfortable in the new environment and develop higher levels of English language proficiency
Difficulty observing school/class expectations	Unfamiliarity with formal schooling and classroom expectations is often experienced by children new to U.S. schools; they require additional time and support to become more accustomed to U.S. schools' behavioral and learning expectations
Preferences in style(s) of learning	Preferred styles of learning are reflective of cultural values and styles of ELLs may be different than typically emphasized in school
Difficulty learning through teaching/ classroom strategies	Teaching strategies typically used in today's classrooms may conflict with cultural views and/or be inappropriate for student's limited English language proficiency levels

Source: Adapted from Berger (2000); Baca & Cervantes (2004); Collier & Hoover (1987); Cummins (1984); Hoover & Collier (1985); Jerrell (2000); Ortiz & Wilkinson (1990).

difference and a learning disability is that a disability is represented by characteristics that limit or interfere with one's learning, often regardless of the instructional method used, while cultural and linguistic diversity or difference is a strength that advances and supports students' educational progress when students receive appropriate instruction. During the multi-level instructional process, educators should document the results of efforts undertaken to differentiate between a difference and a disability as it pertains to the educational needs of ELLs. To best determine difference from disability, educators at a minimum must

1. Make certain that various evidence-based interventions have been tried

2. Engage in culturally/linguistically appropriate interventions with ELLs

3. Develop and use effective decision making strategies and practices to make team decisions

4. Ensure that team members are sufficiently prepared to make informed data-driven decisions about ELLs and their needs using all available and relevant progress monitoring data

Gathering Relevant Student Data

Along with objective data, information gathered on ELLs' academic and social-emotional abilities and needs must be valid and corroborated. To address this area of need, Wilkinson, Ortiz, and Robertson-Courtney (2004) conducted a study in which an expert panel reviewed documents and records of ELLs identified as having a learning disability. These results are directly applicable to multi-tiered instructional decision making.

The expert panel reviewed the documents to determine if the identified students qualified as having learning disabilities, as recommended by the special education placement team. They considered various items within the records including language assessments, standardized test results, IQ and achievement test results, and statements describing discrepancies between potential and actual achievement. Results from the study revealed that the panel agreed that slightly over half of the ELLs clearly qualified for special education, while the others did not qualify. Within the qualified group, the panel questioned the classification of some of the students as having a learning disability and suggested that more data were required to make a more informed disability decision. For those students who did not appear to qualify for special education, the panel found one or more of the following:

1. Significant events (e.g., divorce, death in family) in the child's life affecting education were not considered in eligibility decisions

2. Records contained missing or incomplete data upon which eligibility decisions were made

3. Inappropriate assessments, particularly assessing the students in their nondominant language, which yielded invalid results;

4. Prereferral interventions were either not completed or results not documented for consideration in eligibility decisions

Implications for Multi-Tiered Instruction

Results of this study encourage practitioners to ensure that the proper information about ELLs is gathered and used in making tiered instructional decisions, specifically attending to the above four items (Willkinson, Ortiz, & Robertson-Courtney, 2004). Additional suggestions from this study are presented later in this chapter.

Evidence-Based Interventions and Multi-Tiered Instruction

Evidence-based interventions are instructional practices that have been researched and validated for their intended purposes and population of learners. As discussed, the use of evidence-based interventions is central to the effective implementation of multi-tiered instruction. Also included is the idea that the interventions must be implemented the way they were designed and researched (i.e., implementation with fidelity). To ensure proper implementation of evidence-based interventions with ELLs, the following checklist may be used. The guide, illustrated in Table 5.3, provides several items to consider during the selection and implementation process of evidence-based interventions.

Table 5.3   Selecting Appropriate Evidence-Based Interventions

As evidence-based interventions for an ELL are considered, the following should be completed and addressed to ensure proper selection and use:

___ Student's most proficient language for instruction is identified

___ Student's level of acculturation and adjustment to school environment is determined

___ Discrepancies between teaching and learning style differences are identified

___ Culturally and linguistically relevant instructional interventions are attempted and results documented

___ ESL and/or bilingual education instruction is implemented

___ Sufficient time and opportunity for student to make satisfactory progress are provided relative to acculturation and English proficiency levels

___ Authentic or other criterion-referenced tests are used to assess student progress and socio-emotional development

___ One or more classroom observations are made to observe student interactions in the academic environment and ensure fidelity of implementation of interventions

Source: Adapted from Hoover (2001).

The purpose of the checklist is to assist educators to ensure selection of the most appropriate evidence-based interventions for ELLs struggling with learning early in the process of identifying needs. For example, parental input into their perceptions of the child's suspected problem may help clarify cultural influences or values taught to the child. Also, classroom observations are necessary to determine how suspected problems are interrelated with various content areas and the extent to which various evidence-based interventions assist with promoting student achievement. Educators should discuss how each of these checklist items has been addressed prior to acting on multi-tiered progress monitoring data.

In addition, educators must ensure that they possess culturally responsive teaching practices to minimize erroneous multi-tiered instructional decision making. Table 5.4 identifies several knowledge and skill areas that educators of ELLs should possess to provide an effective education for ELLs in any tier of instruction. Practitioners should evaluate their own skills and abilities to ensure they possess these needed competencies, or work with an individual who does possess these skills.

Table 5.4　Knowledge and Skills to Ensure Effective Multi-Tiered Instruction for Struggling ELLs

1. Knowledge of the appropriate use of instruments and procedures to assess language proficiency and first and second language abilities

2. Knowledge of the principles needed to select a measure designed for use with students from the target populations, including but not limited to consideration of reliability, validity, norms, standards for administration, interpretation of outcomes, and sources of cultural bias

3. Knowledge of limitations of language assessment that result from examiner role, testing situation, content selection, questioning, dialect varieties of the target language, use of interpretation, and social-emotional factors

4. Ability to apply the information from testing, observations, and parent and teacher interviews to identify (a) baseline levels of skills and comprehension, (b) conditions under which skill acquisition can occur most efficiently, (c) the sequence of instructional activities needed, and (d) a plan for evaluation of both process and performance objectives

5. Knowledge and application of appropriate collaboration skills related to working with educational staff and parents in planning and implementing individual educational plans for students demonstrating a disability

6. Ability to devise or adapt existing instruments for assessing students which may include (a) developing new normative data appropriate to the population and (b) developing informal instruments appropriate to the population

7. Knowledge of factors that influence second language acquisition, including use, motivation, attitude, personality, cognition, and the first language

8. Knowledge of cognitive and language development of a normally developing student

9. Knowledge of cultural factors, including semantic and pragmatic systems as they relate to sociolinguistic environment (i.e., parent-student, school-student interaction)

10. Knowledge of the dynamics of the interpretation procedure, including but not limited to the establishment of rapport with participants, kinds of information loss inherent in the interpretation procedure, the use of appropriate nonverbal communication, methods and techniques of interpretation, and the importance of obtaining accurate translations.

11. Ability to plan and execute pre and post assessment conferences

Source: Adapted from Hoover (2001).

Multi-Tier Teams and the Decision Making Process

Over the past two decades, researchers have investigated the effectiveness of educational team practices, particularly as they relate to referral to special education. While decision making teams continue to evolve as multi-tiered instruction expands in our schools, it is crucial that the issues or mistakes made by previous problem-solving teams be minimized. Summary research results suggest that teams often lack clear organization and struggle to make effective decisions (Moore et al. 1998). Klingner and Harry (2004) investigated the effectiveness of child study teams with ELLs and identified several issues that teams must address to provide an effective decision-making process. Table 5.5, developed from information found in Klingner and Harry (2004) and Hoover (2001), includes several selected issues that all problem-solving teams, including multi-tier teams, must consider when addressing the instructional intervention needs of struggling ELLs.

Table 5.5 Issues to Consider in the Multi-Tier Decision Making Process for an English Language Learner

Item	Consideration
Difference Versus Disability	Educators must ensure that limited English proficiency is not mistaken for a learning or language disability.
Proper Time for Formal Referral	Formal referral for special education evaluation should only occur after multi-tiered interventions have been implemented and progress documented.
Proper Language of Instruction/ Assessment	Teams must instruct/assess ELLs in their most proficient language to determine difference from disability.
Limited English Proficiency and IQ	Teams must be cognizant of the fact that limited proficiency in the use of English does not indicate low IQ or inability to use higher order thinking abilities.
Opportunities to Learn	Teams must ensure that students with limited English proficiency are provided sufficient opportunities to learn by implementing necessary accommodations to address cultural and linguistic differences.
Cross-Cultural Observations/ Interviews	Teams must ensure that observations and interviews conducted with ELLs are culturally and linguistically appropriate.
Proper Interpretation and Use of Progress-Monitoring Data	Teams must corroborate progress data with authentic, classroom-based information, observations, and interviews.

As shown, seven specific issues are identified along with special considerations for ELLs. Issues include determining the most appropriate time to refer a student, recognizing that limited English proficiency is *not* synonymous with lower intelligence, and differentiating between a learning difference and a learning disability. To further assist multi-tier team practitioners to provide the most meaningful intervention process for ELLs, a checklist, also developed from information found in Klingner and Harry (2004) and Hoover (2001), is provided in Table 5.6.

Table 5.6   Multi-Tier Team Checklist for English Language Learners

Instructions: Place a check next to each item when it is addressed by the team for an English language learner. Record any related comments below each item:

___ Evidence-based interventions are implemented and progress is monitored.
Comments:

___ Culturally responsive team decision making strategies were used.
Comments:

___ Parent interactions were encouraged and valued.
Comments:

___ Cultural and linguistic factors relative to suspected problem area were addressed.
Comments:

___ Referral for formal special education evaluation made at appropriate time and only after several evidence-based interventions have been attempted.
Comments:

___ Learning differences versus learning disabilities were discussed.
Comments:

___ Translator was used properly when necessary.
Comments:

___ Classroom observations were completed.
Comments:

___ Effects of limited English proficiency on student's ability to learn curriculum content and skills were considered.
Comments:

As shown, the checklist contains nine critical items necessary to ensure the most appropriate multi-tiered process for ELLs and assist teams to make the most effective decisions concerning level and intensity of interventions.

Nondiscriminatory Progress Monitoring

One of the more controversial issues in the education of students from culturally and linguistically diverse backgrounds pertains to the use of biased assessment instruments and associated practices. According to Baca and Clark (1992), 25 percent of bias is found in the assessment instruments and 75 percent of bias is found in the interpretation and use of assessment results. While advances have been made to ensure that assessment and progress monitoring instruments have minimal bias, assessment practices for ELLs still contain a variety of biases that affect progress monitoring results. In addition, as previously discussed, interventions and practices during Tier 1 instruction may have a significant impact on future decisions within the multi-tiered process. As a result, attention to nondiscriminatory progress monitoring used with struggling ELLs must begin during Tier 1 instruction and continue throughout the entire multi-tier decision making process.

Nondiscriminatory assessment practices include a variety of tasks, and practitioners must be cognizant of the fact that some progress monitoring practices may not be appropriate for use with culturally and linguistically diverse students since they may yield unreliable and invalid results. During the progress monitoring process, two of the more important issues challenging ELLs are (a) opportunities to learn and (b) the language in which the evidence-based intervention is delivered. One way to ensure that progress monitoring with ELLs is valid and reliable is to evaluate the process by adhering to various nondiscriminatory practices. Several important considerations for nondiscriminatory practices have been identified for practitioners working with ELLs (Figueroa & Newsome, 2004). Table 5.7, developed from information found in the Figueroa and Newsome study and Hoover et al. (2008), provides a summary of items reflective of nondiscriminatory practices, which must be considered during progress-monitoring activities.

This guide should be used by practitioners, in conjunction with the other recommended guides in this chapter, as a means to provide an appropriate progress-monitoring process for ELLs. Adhering to these items will lead to more effective and accurate decision making within the multi-tiered instructional process.

Table 5.7   Guide to Nondiscriminatory Progress Monitoring

Tasks reflecting nondiscriminatory practices . . .

1. Cross cultural interviews and classroom observations are conducted.

2. Cross-validation of information from the home and family settings corroborates progress monitored data.

3. Culturally responsive progress-monitoring methods are implemented.

4. Effects of environmental and cultural influences on suspected problem are documented.

5. Progress monitoring is completed by culturally and/or linguistically competent persons.

6. Linguistically appropriate goals and services are included in progress monitoring.

7. Previous instructional programs and student progress in those programs are considered.

8. Evidence-based adaptive behavior interventions are attempted and documented.

9. Home and family information is documented and accurate.

10. Student's language dominance and English proficiency are determined.

11. Translators/Interpreters are properly used if necessary in the progress monitoring.

12. Alternative and authentic forms of progress monitoring are included.

Source: Adapted from Hoover (2001).

MAKING ACCURATE MULTI-TIERED DATA-DRIVEN DECISIONS

Concluding Recommendations

As previously discussed, Wilkinson, Ortiz, and Robertson-Courtney (2004) investigated the link between student data and decisions made by problem-solving teams, specifically for special education. The researchers concluded that important background educational needs and characteristics are frequently overlooked by teams. Characteristics such as home language, oral language proficiency, previous instruction, and literacy abilities in both first and second languages were overlooked (Wilkinson, Ortiz, & Robertson-Courtney, 2004). This study also concluded, as did the studies conducted by Klingner and Harry (2004) and Figueroa and Newsome (2004), that assessment personnel must be better prepared to monitor ELLs' progress to make accurate data-driven instructional decisions for struggling learners.

To assist teams to make more informed decisions, Wilkinson and Ortiz (2004) and Ortiz (2002) identified several skill areas important for practitioners to possess. These are particularly important in the education of ELLs within multi-tiered instruction. Skills these authors discussed include ability to

1. Efficiently manage large amounts of information on ELLs

2. Provide early intervening services by differentiating general class curriculum to meet specific needs

3. Effectively use problem-solving skills to best select evidence-based interventions bearing in mind several critical aspects (e.g., type of intervention, duration, monitoring response to the intervention)

4. Differentiate instruction to address cultural and linguistic needs

5. Interpret progress monitoring data to consider alternate reasons for suspected problems (e.g., acculturation; lack of sufficient opportunities to learn; impact of limited English proficiency on curriculum performance)

6. Corroborate progress monitoring results using culturally and linguistically relevant practices and devices

As suggested by Wilkinson, Ortiz, and Robertson-Courtney (2004), a variety of sources are needed to sufficiently understand an ELL's suspected learning problem and to make accurate progress monitoring decisions. Educator teams responsible for making multi-tier intervention decisions must use all available information, as well as make certain to gather other necessary data to acquire a comprehensive understanding of the student (Wilkinson, Ortiz, & Robertson-Courtney, 2004).

SUMMARY

The significance of effective multi-tiered evidence-based interventions, appropriate progress monitoring, and effective data-driven decision making practices cannot be overstated when addressing the needs of ELLs struggling in learning. This chapter discussed many issues associated with the overall process associated with the education of struggling ELLs. Several guides and checklists were presented to assist practitioners to ensure that cultural and linguistic factors and issues are appropriately explored, discussed, and accounted for during the comprehensive implementation of multi-tiered interventions in school districts nationwide. The use and application of the information discussed in this chapter will assist problem-solving teams to make more informed decisions, based on appropriate and objective data, concerning language differences and language disabilities in English language learners.

6 Considerations When Assessing ELLs for Special Education

John J. Hoover and Laura Méndez Barletta

As discussed in Chapter 5, a variety of progress-monitoring practices must be undertaken to best meet the needs of ELLs who show initial signs of struggling with learning. Also, as previously discussed in Chapter 3, students who do not demonstrate adequate progress toward curricular benchmarks through the use of evidence-based interventions in RTI may eventually be referred for special education evaluation and possible placement. In addition to various cultural and linguistic considerations discussed in the previous chapter, to reduce measurement error, other factors must also be addressed in the formal assessment of ELLs suspected of having a disability. An underlying assumption when assessing ELLs is that every effort must be made to ensure that learning characteristics and behaviors are assessed, observed, and interpreted appropriately to avoid misplacement into special education. This is essential in the assessment process to avoid misinterpreting language acquisition as learning disabilities (LD).

Student assessment plays a central role in the education of ELLs in multi-tiered response to intervention to meet a variety of purposes, including

- aiding teachers in monitoring students' language development (in their first and/or second language)
- helping teachers to monitor the quality and progress of students' day-to-day academic and social emotional learning

- placement of students in, or exit from, special programs such as bilingual education, English as a second language, special education, and gifted and talented programs

Different states and school districts use various methods to assess ELLs. That is, they use methods such as home language surveys, observations, interviews, referrals, grades, and formal testing to place and monitor students' progress in special programs. It is important to note that when ELLs are tested to determine their English language proficiency or academic achievement in English, the tests tend to be administered in English. More often than not, ELLs do not fully understand test instructions or the tests themselves (Zehler, Hopstock, Fleishman, & Greniuk, 1994). When an achievement test is administered in a language a child does not fully understand, the test becomes a language test rather than a test of knowledge of subject area content or skill.

ELL CLASSIFICATION ISSUES AND SPECIAL EDUCATION ELIGIBILITY

Researchers have expressed concerns over the validity of special education assessments and classification procedures for ELLs that affect both instruction and assessment decisions. However, ELL students with lower levels of English proficiency may experience a more critical problem. These students may be misidentified as students with LD, since deficiencies in English may be misinterpreted as a sign of LD or reading disabilities (Abedi, 2004a). The following challenges contribute to the problematic nature of ELL assessment:

- Language factors that affect the performance of ELLs may also influence the performance of students with LD.
- Similarities between language background characteristics and the level of English proficiency may make ELL students with lower levels of English particularly vulnerable for misclassification in learning and/or reading disabilities.
- Misrepresentation is significant for ELLs, and educators must better understand the role of language in assessments conducted in English to ensure reliable and valid testing results.

Overall, educators conducting a formal assessment of an ELL for special education, including within the RTI process, must keep in mind the following general testing characteristics:

1. ELLs generally perform lower than non-ELLs on content-based assessments (i.e., math, science, social sciences), even though they might not actually know less.

2. English language proficiency affects instruction and assessment.

3. Language background variables may confound ELLs' content-based assessment outcomes.

4. Assessments for ELL students have lower validity and reliability, particularly for those at the lower end of the English proficiency spectrum (Abedi, 2004a).

5. Language factors may be a source of measurement error, affecting validity and reliability (Messick, 1989).

Formal assessment for ELLs for possible special education must therefore consider several key areas to ensure effective decision-making concerning differences between learning and language disabilities. These include

- linguistic features
- dialect and register
- linguistic misalignment

Students with LD as well as ELLs (particularly those at the lower level of English proficiency distribution) may have more difficulty with test items that have unfamiliar words and/or a complex linguistic structure.

Linguistic Features

A variety of linguistic features can impact assessment results for ELLs. When considering the needs of ELLs, reliable and valid assessment results are critical to making sound educational decisions. Assessment is *reliable* if it produces consistent results. A *valid* assessment occurs when the assessment measures what it purports to measure (Best & Kahn, 1998). Various linguistic features may impact formal assessment results, especially comprehension, and must be considered in the special education decision-making process as illustrated in Table 6.1.

Lack of familiarity with these linguistic features will generate unreliable and invalid test results as the test taker inaccurately interprets test items.

Dialect and Register

Dialect and register are as important as overall language abilities in affecting the validity of measures of academic achievement for ELLs

Table 6.1 Special Considerations When Interpreting Linguistic Features in the Comprehension of ELLs

Feature	Description	Special Considerations
Word frequency/familiarity	Words most frequently used in reading /spoken language	Words high on a general frequency list for English are likely to be familiar to most readers because they are encountered often. Readers who encounter familiar words are more likely to interpret them quickly and correctly, having a positive impact on comprehension and test results
Word length	Use of single syllable to multisyllable words	Words tend to be longer as their frequency of use decreases. In one study, language minority students performed better on math test items with shorter word lengths than items with longer word lengths.
Sentence length	Use of two–three word sentences through lengthy multi-word sentences	The length of a sentence serves as an index for its complexity and can be used to predict comprehension difficulty.
Passive/Active voice	Use of passive vs. active structure (e.g., Active–"Juan hit the ball"; Passive–"The ball was hit by Juan.")	Passive constructions can be especially challenging to nonnative English speakers.
Long noun phrases	Sentences that contain several interconnected phrases requiring learners to comprehend more complex sentences	Noun phrases with several modifiers provide a potential source of difficulty in test items. Romance languages (e.g., Spanish, French, Italian, Portuguese) make less use of compounding than English.
Long question phrases	Questions that contain longer phrases and numerous words	Longer question phrases occur less frequently than short question phrases. Low-frequency expressions (long question phrases) are often harder to read/understand.
Comparative structures	Comparing/Contrasting ideas	Comparative constructions often represent potential sources of difficulty for nonnative speakers as well as for speakers of nonmainstream dialects.

Term	Description	Notes
Prepositional phrases	Phrases within a sentence that begin with a preposition	Students may experience difficulty with prepositions. English and Spanish may differ in their use of prepositions.
Sentence and discourse structure	Complexities of words/phrases used in a sentence or group of sentences	Although sentences may have a similar number of words, one may be more difficult to understand due to syntax complexities or discourse relationships among sentences.
Subordinate clause	Clauses in sentences designed to show relationships and connect ideas that do not stand alone	For many students, subordinate clauses may increase the complexity of the sentence generating confusion or lack of understanding.
Relative clauses	Clauses that characterize (e.g., "The dog, who loves bones, barked for a treat.")	Relative clauses are less frequent in spoken English than in written English and some students may have limited exposure to them and their usage in writing/reading.
Concrete vs. abstract presentations	Use of concrete examples or statements, avoiding the use of vague abstractions	Students tend to perform better when content is presented in concrete rather than abstract terms.
Negation	Use of negatives such as no, not none, never in sentences	Sentences that contain negations are more difficult to understand than affirmative sentences. In Spanish, double negative constructions retain a negative meaning, rather an affirmative meaning as in English.

Source: Adapted from Abedi (2004b); Abedi et al. (1997); Adams (1990); Celce-Murcia & Larsen-Freeman (1983); Cummins, Kintsch, Reusser, & Spanos et al., (1998); Freeman (1978); Hunt (1965); Mestre (1988); Orr (1987) Slobin (1968).

(Solano-Flores, 2004). Since dialect and register cannot be disassociated from language, testing policies and practices for ELLs must consider these varieties of language in order to make more substantial progress toward the use of valid and fair measures to assess ELLs' academic achievement.

Dialect and Language

Dialect is a variation of a language used by a subset of a larger population who share a common language. Dialects are different ways of expressing the same idea as they reflect the social structure (e.g., class, gender, and origin). Every language has different dialects or varieties. Every version of a language is a dialect. In other words, standard English is a dialect. Linguists define dialect as a variety of a language that is distinguished from other varieties of the same language through use of pronunciation, grammar, vocabulary, discourse conventions, and other linguistic features (Solano-Flores, 2004). Dialects pertain to the linguistic and cultural characteristics of the students who belong to the same broad linguistic group. Dialects are governed by defined systems whose deviations from other dialects of the same language are systematic rather than random (Crystal, 1997). For example, a soft drink may be referred to as "soda," "pop," "soft drink," or the brand name of the product. In another example, an automobile may be referred to as "wheels," "car," or "auto" by different people living in different parts of the country.

Influence of Dialect in the Assessment of ELLs

- While the term *dialect* often refers to the language used by people from a particular geographic or social group or to mean a substandard variety of a language, *everyone* speaks a dialect (Preston, 1993).
- Standard English is one of many recognized English dialects (i.e., variations within the English language occurs based on factors such as region of the country or socioeconomic status; Wardhaugh, 2002).
- The origins of variations in dialects stem, in part, from contact with other languages or from specific features of a language shared by its speakers (Wolfram, 2000).
- Linguists note that several nonstandard English dialects are "as complex and as regularly patterned as other varieties of English, which are considered more standard" (Farr & Ball, 1999, p. 206).
- The dialect associated with a form of spoken English by African Americans, African American Vernacular English (AAVE), contains language structures similar in complexity to standard English dialect.

Register and Language

Register refers to a variation of a language determined by situation or context. Registers are ways of saying different things; they reflect social processes. A register is the words and patterns of usage that the members of a particular culture or group typically associate with a specific context. It is language used for a specific purpose. For example, baseball players share a common set of terms and way of talking, or register, about their sport. A "bag," "plate," and "strike" mean something different when talking about a baseball game than when discussing shopping, doing the dishes, or boycotting work. A situation, and its associated register, may vary in degree of specificity. The register is recognized as a specific selection of words, structures, and even body language; however, a register is defined in terms of meanings (Halliday, 1978). As related to student assessment, registers have to do with academic language and the contexts in which students receive instruction or are tested through the use of language.

Influence of Register in the Assessment of ELLs

- ELLs' responses to assessment items vary across items and languages (Solano-Flores, 2004).
- ELLs' linguistic proficiencies vary tremendously across language modes (i.e., writing, reading, listening, speaking) and contexts (e.g., at home, at school, with friends, with relatives).
- ELLs' linguistic proficiencies are shaped by schooling (e.g., bilingual or full immersion programs) and the way in which language instruction is implemented (e.g., by emphasizing reading or writing in one language or the other) (Genesee, 1994; Valdés & Figueroa, 1994).
- Students might perform better in their first language than in English for some test items but better in English than in their first language for other items.

Therefore, when assessing ELLs, practitioners should determine

1. English language proficiency

2. Native language proficiency

3. Content area strengths/weaknesses in *each* language

4. The student's experiential background

5. Ways in which language instruction has been implemented with the student

In regards to dialect, when assessing ELLs, practitioners must

1. Know that whenever ELLs are tested (in any language) *some* dialect of that language is being tested (most often the standard form of the language)

2. Consider the student's pronunciation, grammar, and vocabulary features, which may differ from those of other students who speak the same language, but a different dialect

3. Identify the linguistic and cultural characteristics of the learner

4. Remember that the dialect of the language in which students are tested is a powerful influence that shapes student performance

5. Understand that knowing more about a student's dialect is crucial to obtaining valid academic achievement test results (Solano-Flores, 2004)

In regards to register, when assessing ELLs, practitioners should consider the extent to which the learner is familiar with

1. *Semantics* (e.g., "root" has different meanings in colloquial language and in mathematics), word frequency (e.g., "ion" is mostly restricted to the content of science)

2. *Idiomatic expressions* (e.g., the option "None of the above" is a phrase used almost exclusively in multiple choice tests)

3. *Notation* (e.g., "A divided by B is represented as A/B")

4. *Conventions* (e.g., uppercase letters are used to denote variables); syntactical structures (e.g., the structure of multiple choice items in which an incomplete sentence—the stem—is followed by several phrases—the options)

5. *Ways of building arguments* (e.g., "Let A be an integer number")

Linguistic Misalignment

Linguistic misalignment is defined as the mismatch between the features of the dialect and the register used in a test, and the features of the dialect and the register used by students (Solano-Flores, 2004). An example of this type of misalignment may be found in a word or a syntactical structure on a test that is uncommon in the dialect and register used by the student being assessed. It is important for practitioners to keep in mind that while one or two misalignments will not necessarily affect student performance, multiple misalignment instances in the same test can have significant detrimental effects on test results for ELLs (Solano-Flores, 2004). Solano-Flores (2004) described two dimensions of linguistic misalignment, frequency and criticality:

> *Frequency* refers to the number of instances of misalignment (e.g., an unfamiliar idiomatic expression, a word of low frequency in the student's dialect, a slight variation in a notation convention), which can range from none to many.

> *Criticality* refers to the importance of instances of misalignment, which can range from trivial to significant.

Test items are likely to be *linguistically sound* when there are few or mild instances of linguistic misalignment. Items are likely to be linguistically challenging when there are many unimportant instances of linguistic misalignment—each of which would not affect the student's performance by itself—or when there are few but severe instances of linguistic misalignment (Solano-Flores, 2004).

Test items can also be thought of as unintended samples of dialect and register. When either too many mild or too few but severe instances of linguistic misalignment occur, the likelihood increases that an item affects performance due to language. However, given its significance, linguistic misalignment is extremely difficult to predict with judgmental methods. Table 6.2 provides a survey for educators to use as an initial guide to determine the appropriateness of an assessment device based on language, dialect, and register factors discussed in this chapter.

As shown, a variety of factors are included and the more of these that exist as "yes" the more confident the tester may be in accommodating language, dialect, and register in the assessment process for ELLs. In addition, one strategy for addressing linguistic misalignment consists of ensuring that the number of items included in a test is large enough to ensure that language will not be a source of measurement error in spite of the fact that some of the linguistic features of the test represent instances of misalignment (Solano-Flores, 2004).

In summary, many concerns over the reliability and validity of assessments for ELLs are due, in part, to students' lack of familiarity with the linguistic features embedded in English tests. One reason it is so challenging to assess ELLs accurately is that the field has not yet developed a precise

Table 6.2   Survey for Determining Linguistic Appropriateness of Assessment Device

Item	Response	
	Yes	No
Test language is similar to instructional language	Y	N
Test norms reflect a variety of dialects within the language spoken by the test taker	Y	N
The Standard Dialect used in the test is determined to be the most socially acceptable dialect in the language of the test (e.g., Spanish; Haitian-Creole)	Y	N
The dialect of the language found in the test is compatible with the dialect used by the test taker	Y	N
Test avoids the use of colloquial terms with unusual meanings	Y	N
Word meanings found on a test are similar to their use in colloquial language	Y	N
Test taker understands meaning of expressions typically found only in tests (e.g., "none of the above")	Y	N
Test questions are not in conflict with previous school experiences of test taker (e.g., understands the difference between a comma and a decimal point)	Y	N
The number of test items with unfamiliar expressions is low	Y	N
Summary of Scoring: Number Identified as: _____ Y (Yes) _____N (No)		

Source: Adapted from Solano-Flores (2004).

test of language proficiency (Langdon, 1989; Ortiz, 1997). A related challenge is that the accuracy of the information about an ELL's language background obtained from a Home Language Survey may be suspect, since inconsistent information may be provided by the parents for a variety of reasons, including concerns over equity of opportunity for their children, citizenship issues and immigration status, and the literacy of the parent (Abedi, 2004b).

Implications for Assessment

Assessment tools that have complex linguistic structures may provide inaccurate results for ELLs (Abedi, 2004a). Table 6.3 provides a survey for educators to use to identify students' experiential backgrounds with linguistic features found in assessment devices.

Table 6.3   Guide to Determining Experiential Background With Assessment
                  Linguistic Features

Feature	None	Little	Some	Extensive
Word frequency/familiarity (English words high on a general frequency list)	1	2	3	4
Word length (Longer versus shorter word lengths)	1	2	3	4
Sentence length (Longer versus shorter sentences)	1	2	3	4
Passive voice constructions (Exposure to passive voice)	1	2	3	4
Long noun phrases (Noun phrases with several modifiers)	1	2	3	4
Long question phrases (Longer rather than shorter question phrases)	1	2	3	4
Prepositional phrases (Interpretation of prepositions)	1	2	3	4
Sentence and discourse structure (Syntactic structure or discourse relationships among sentences)	1	2	3	4
Subordinate clause (Clause in a sentence that cannot stand alone)	1	2	3	4
Relative clauses (A dependent clause Introduced by a relative pronoun)	1	2	3	4
Concrete vs. abstract/impersonal presentations (Abstract versus concrete and expository versus narrative)	1	2	3	4
Negation (Sentences containing negations, e.g., no, not, none, never)	1	2	3	4

Source: Adapted from Abedi (2004a).

The reliability of the commonly used standardized assessments in content-based areas may be negatively affected by the complex linguistic structure of test items, such as those presented in the above guide. Decisions based on the results of formal special education assessments, including those made within RTI, may be problematic for ELL students and other subgroups of students who may have language deficiencies and lack familiarity with these linguistic features.

As a result, assessment of ELLs for special education must include the use of authentic assessment to best understand their linguistic features and educational needs.

AUTHENTIC ASSESSMENT

Special educators are often not well informed when assessing learners who primarily speak a language other than English, or whose ethnic and linguistic backgrounds differ significantly from mainstream English speakers (Barrera, 2004). Second language learners may display learning characteristics very similar to their peers with LD. Like students with LD, they might exhibit severe discrepancies between academic potential and actual achievement, and severe underachievement. Because ELLs are likely to come from diverse cultural and linguistic backgrounds or lack exposure to schooling, their learning difficulties can be mistaken for deeper cognitive deficits. A variety of authentic assessment practices are appropriate for helping to differentiate between a difference and disability and are often preferable to traditional approaches. The current emphasis on RTI also provides a structure for facilitating the use of authentic assessments within a structure designed to provide prevention and intervention services to students. Two of these authentic approaches particularly useful when assessing ELLs within the overall structure of RTI include curriculum-based assessment/measurement and dynamic assessment. Curriculum-based and "dynamic" assessments are two approaches considered critical in assessment for identification and instruction among second language learners (Barrera, 2004). That is, these approaches may help educators using Tier 1 and Tier 2 interventions, which precede formal eligibility/identification procedures for special education.

Curriculum-Based Assessment/Measurement

Curriculum-based assessment (CBA) comes in two forms: a nonstandardized form (CBA) where teachers use classroom-based tasks to determine student capabilities, and a standardized form (CBM—curriculum-based measurement) where specific learning tasks are tested for reliability and validity. In CBA, a teacher takes work samples from the student in the area being assessed using tasks and content the student has encountered in the classroom (Barrera, 2004). In CBM, specific basic skills tasks have been validated with other measures of achievement. In CBA and CBM, the teacher (1) determines a student's current ability, (2) determines a possible intervention to address a specific content and/or skill, (3) conducts an intervention to teach the content and/or skill, and (4) tests the student to monitor progress.

More specifically, teachers tend to use CBA to monitor student progress and use the data from these assessments to plan and modify instruction. One benefit of using CBA with ELLs is they are tested on material they are exposed to in the classroom (as opposed to standardized tests). In addition, the use of CBA may allow teachers to create linguistically and culturally appropriate/relevant assessment tools for ELL students. The use of CBM, on the other hand, allows teachers to monitor students' educational progress by directly assessing their academic skills. Although most research on CBM has been conducted with native English speakers, the use of CBM may also help determine how well ELLs are acquiring English skills and content area material.

Although curriculum-based assessments/measurements are considered a "mainstream" component of special education practice, there are significant gaps in empirical testing using CBA/Ms with English language learners. In other words, results may be difficult to interpret when determining whether a second language learner has a disability. For example, if a second language learner is asked to read a passage, one will not know from the data whether low fluency and accuracy scores result from a lack of reading experience, language, content experience, or a suspected disability (Barrera, 2004). In this instance, additional authentic assessment is warranted to further clarify potential disability from difference, such as dynamic assessment.

Dynamic Assessment

Many assessment approaches can be problematic when applied to the specific needs of second language learners suspected of having disabilities. Barrera (2004) argues that dynamic assessment is a promising practice for distinguishing between disability-related learning difficulties and the normal process of acquiring a new language. Dynamic assessment examines students' learning ability as a function of what learners can do as they are being taught rather than of what students already know or do not know. Dynamic assessment procedures consist of teaching a new learning task to a student and collecting progress and procedural data as the student learns the new task. Thus, dynamic assessment is less dependent on the student's previous opportunities to learn than other assessment procedures (e.g., standardized assessment tests).

Effectiveness of Dynamic Assessment With English Language Learners

To illustrate the effectiveness of dynamic assessment, Barrera (2004) conducted a study where 38 teachers from general and special education were recruited to conduct assessments of 114 work samples from three groups of Mexican American students from two school districts in southwestern Minnesota and south Texas. The groups were designated as follows: (1) second language learners identified with LD, (2) second language learning peers not in special education, and (3) peers considered normal to high achieving bilingual or English-proficient. The dynamic assessment procedure consisted of using a two-entry "reflection and analysis" journal to have students write notes as they learned vocabulary terms. Students were taught to use the "reflection" side of the journal to engage in vocabulary building activities before, during, and after classroom discussions or lectures. In the "analysis" side of the journal, students wrote vocabulary definitions in their own words and constructed two sentences using the vocabulary words.

The process of dynamic assessment consisted of three steps. First, teachers asked students to take notes to determine if they had already acquired the skill to be taught. Second, students were provided continuous instruction on how to use the two-entry journal during a two-week period. Finally, a posttest on the new skill consisted of the last instance of journal note taking without instruction on the final day of the two-week period (Barrera, 2004). Teachers involved in the study conducted masked assessments of student work samples (i.e., they did not know in which group each student belonged). More specifically, a packet was given to each teacher that included three sets of student work samples previously coded by group (LEP with LD, LEP only, and bilingual/ English-proficient). Further, four sets of scoring sheets were provided for each set of student notes. Teachers then reviewed the notes to see to what degree students followed directions for completing the dynamic assessment. Results from Barrera's study indicate that learners with limited English proficiency and LD can be differentiated through data collected from dynamic assessments and assessed by classroom teachers (2004). Furthermore, results indicate that high achieving learners had a higher percentage of key words with notes (in their journals) than LEP and LEP/LD groups, but general education students demonstrated the lowest percentage. However, high achieving learners were the least likely to complete the task of writing two sentences.

Results of Barrera's study also show that many of the measures used did not demonstrate statistically significant differences among students with limited English proficiency and their peers with limited English proficiency and LD. Barrera (2004) notes that differentiation among the student groups was clearest with quantitative measures (e.g., words and letters written, percentage of words spelled correctly, number of complete sentences). Barrera argues that this general outcome verifies the difficulties observed in the field for clearly differentiating low-achieving learners from those with

LD and reinforces the views of researchers and practitioners seeking more objective, quantifiable methods for assessing these learners. See Table 6.4 for a summary of key findings from this research.

Table 6.4   Summary of Dynamic Assessment Research Findings

1. Learners with limited English proficiency (LEP) and LD can be differentiated through data collected from dynamic assessments.

2. High achieving learners had a higher percentage of key words with notes than LEP and LEP/LD groups, but general education students demonstrated the lowest percentage.

3. High achieving learners completed the task to write two sentences with a lower percentage.

4. Many of the measures used did not demonstrate statistically significant differences among students with limited English proficiency and their peers with limited English proficiency and LD.

5. High achieving learners usually out-performed others despite their predilection to minimize their efforts in the writing of notes.

6. General education students showed minimal total writing.

7. Students with limited English proficiency and LD tended to write more total notes despite lower quality of results.

Overall, benefits exist for using curriculum-based assessment/measurement and dynamic and authentic assessment procedures to help distinguish between those students who have true disabilities and those who are struggling for other reasons. Results from these authentic assessment practices provide valuable supplemental progress monitoring and formal assessment results when considering an ELL for possible special education.

SUMMARY

A major source of measurement error in assessment leading to invalid results is produced by the interaction of the student with the test item, and language, or the interaction of the student with the test item, and dialect. Additionally, assessment features designed for native English speakers may pose significant problems for ELLs. ELLs often perform well on some items administered in one language or dialect, and well on other items administered in the other language or dialect. The concept of dialect is relevant to addressing the tremendous linguistic and cultural diversity that may exist within broad linguistic groups of ELLs who are users of the same given language. The concept of register is relevant to addressing academic language and the wide diversity of instructional and assessment contexts. Language factors that affect the dependability of achievement measures vary at the level of dialect. No matter what language any individual speaks (either a first or second language), that person is using a particular dialect (standard or nonstandard) of that language.

Regardless of whether ELLs are tested in English or in their native language, linguistic misalignment occurs when the linguistic features of a test do not match their actual linguistic backgrounds and the contexts within which they have been instructed. This misalignment accounts for measurement error, due to dialect and/or register, and results in less valid assessment results. Linguistic features must be identified and accounted for to obtain accurate, valid, and reliable results for ELLs, particularly those with suspected LD. The use of authentic assessment procedures such as curriculum-based assessment/measurement and dynamic assessment may assist practitioners in the implementation of a more culturally/linguistically appropriate assessment process as ELLs are considered for possible special education due to continued lack of academic progress.

7 Conclusion

Putting the Pieces Together

Leonard M. Baca, Todd Fletcher, and John J. Hoover

INTRODUCTION

This practical book provides teachers of English language learners who struggle with reading with a foundation to make more informed decisions pertaining to understanding English language acquisition and learning disabilities. This, in turn, provides educators with greater knowledge to draw upon to more accurately distinguish language differences from suspected learning disabilities. The intent of this final chapter is to summarize key ideas and practices discussed in the earlier chapters to assist educators of ELLs to integrate information and skills as they move forward with the challenging task of effectively teaching linguistically diverse learners. The previous chapters discussed several key ideas and practices important to bear in mind to best understand language development and learning disabilities. We begin by presenting common themes among the interrelated topics discussed throughout this book.

Universal Screening

All students are screened to determine those who are experiencing academic or behavioral difficulties. Universal screening generally occurs between one and three times per year (IRIS Center for Training Enhancements). When implemented on a periodic basis throughout the academic year (e.g., three times per year, at the beginning, middle, and near end of the school year), students who begin to struggle during the school year who did not demonstrate problems at the beginning of the school year are more quickly identified. Students who fall below a specified cut-off score are identified as struggling learners and provided supplemental support. According to Brown-Chidsey and Steege (2005), many districts use the 25th percentile as the cut-off for determining students at-risk who require additional support.

Progress Monitoring

Struggling learners identified through universal screening are provided supplemental or intensive support to address their needs (i.e., Tier 2 or Tier 3 interventions). The implementation of this supplemental instruction must now also include ongoing progress monitoring, documenting the extent to which students make progress toward the achievement of defined goals. Progress data are gathered on a frequent basis (e.g., monthly, weekly) and should be charted to visually display student progress (Brown-Chidsey & Steege, 2005; Deno, 2005). These data are subsequently used to make informed data-driven decisions reflecting student response to instruction.

Formal Assessment

Formal diagnostic assessment should focus on strengths in both languages, or in the case of simultaneous bilinguals, assessment of the combined use of two languages, which often yields more accurate results than separate assessment within each language. Both curriculum-based measurement and dynamic assessment should be employed in the progress-monitoring and formal assessment stages. To best understand language acquisition, both dialect and register need to be considered in instruction and assessment decisions.

Evidence-Based Interventions

Evidence-based interventions must have been validated with ELLs to be considered appropriate for this population. Effective instruction for ELLs within a multi-tiered framework should include cultural responsiveness; language development beginning early when a student demonstrates a need; reading instruction that is systematic and explicit; and teachers able to craft respectful, reciprocal, and responsive interactions across diverse cultural settings. In addition, where possible and in accordance with district policies, primary language literacy instruction should be provided.

Teacher Preparation and Professional Development

Teacher preparation should (a) focus on the development of cultural and linguistic competence, (b) be interdisciplinary in nature and focus on the whole child including the affective domain, (c) strive to improve skills of all educators including general and special education classroom teachers, and (d) address diverse learners' needs within a system-wide approach that incorporates a culture of collaboration and continual professional development.

PRACTICAL APPLICATIONS OF SUGGESTED INTERVENTIONS

Each of these themes stresses a critical aspect associated with the successful education of ELLs. Collectively, these represent some of the most important features necessary to consider when discerning differences between language development and learning disabilities. As educators move forward in efforts to meet ELL needs, the many practical suggestions discussed in previous chapters will assist to provide an integrated education to best reduce the misinterpretation of language difference needs as disability needs. Several of the practical ideas previously discussed are summarized below.

Learning Disabilities and English Language Development

Learning disabilities and second language acquisition behaviors may appear similar, which, in turn, may lead to misidentification for special education. To best avoid misidentification, educators should bear in mind that language acquisition is a very complex process and is influenced by a variety of factors, including first language proficiency, cultural values/norms, personality, and acculturation. These and related factors must be considered by practitioners with expertise in second language acquisition and skilled in the implementation of instruction and associated progress monitoring to obtain the most valid educational results for ELLs.

Avoiding Misconceptions About ELLs

Interrelated with an understanding of language development and learning disabilities is the need to avoid misconceptions about ELLs. From a practical perspective, educators should bear in mind the following as previously discussed:

1. Utilize explicit instruction and scaffolding as needed

2. Consider a variety of factors, such as those discussed above, to best understand behaviors

3. Examine and consider one's own cultural assumptions and linguistic knowledge when implementing instruction with ELLs

4. Integrate language goals and objectives into instructional activities and expected outcomes

Overall, to best avoid misconceptions about ELLs, educators must recognize that academic and behavioral outcomes are influenced significantly by the interaction between what the learner brings to the classroom and what the school attempts to offer the learner. An understanding of the compatibility or incompatibility between these is essential to best address ELL needs and avoid misconceptions.

Effective Implementation of RTI With ELLs

As previously discussed, the implementation of RTI and multi-tiered learning holds significant promise for ELLs if certain precautions are addressed. These include the use of evidence-based interventions that have been researched with the target population (i.e., ELLs) along with assurances that teachers implementing RTI (a) are adequately trained, (b) receive necessary support to effectively implement evidence-based interventions, and (c) develop the skills necessary for culturally responsive documentation of student responses to instruction. Unless these and similar practices occur, RTI runs the risk of experiencing a fate similar to that found in many prereferral intervention models (i.e., wait to fail models). The practical application of RTI will only be effective if implemented in culturally and linguistically responsive ways by culturally competent educators.

Putting Effective Literacy Instruction Into Practice

Fundamental to avoiding misinterpretations about language development and disabilities is a working knowledge of the practical application of literacy instruction for ELLs. As previously presented, inadequate opportunities to learn often lead to the misrepresentation of learning differences as disabilities (Klingner & Edwards, 2006). The most effective literacy instruction for ELLs provides the learner with culturally relevant teaching, including recognition of the types of literacy instruction previously experienced by the student. While the greater concern is misinterpreting a learning difference as a disability, it is also important to recognize that some ELLs may truly have a learning disability and require targeted instruction to meet their needs as well. To this end, practitioners should adhere to the following suggestions previously explored in this book:

- build strong positive relationships with learners
- value cultural diversity in teaching and learning
- provide sufficient attention and opportunity to oral language development
- differentiate instruction as necessary to account for diverse needs
- provide explicit instruction, particularly when introducing new concepts
- combine phonological awareness with other reading and English language development activities (whether instruction is in the student's first language or English)
- provide explicit vocabulary instruction to facilitate reading comprehension in students' first language and English
- teach and encourage the use of reading comprehension strategies
- help students develop a strong foundation in their first language as a way to promote literacy in both the native language and English (Klingner, Artiles, & Méndez-Barletta, 2006)

Overall, effective literacy instruction requires practitioners to understand, value, and account for diverse learners' cognitive, academic and social-emotional backgrounds and experiences. This knowledge assists educators to best determine literacy needs and reduces tendencies to misinterpret language differences as learning disabilities.

Role of Data-Driven Decision Making

The implementation of multi-tiered instruction and response to intervention models includes provisions in teaching and learning that address one of the most basic principles of instructional decision making. Specifically, this refers to the use of data, directly reflective of instructional efforts, forming the foundation for making decisions concerning tiers and intensity of evidence-based interventions. While RTI problem-solving teams may use several sources of information to make decisions (e.g., teacher ratings, classroom observations, interviews), the use of quantitative data, collected and charted over time, is essential to determining the extent to which a learner responds to instruction. Practitioners in today's classrooms must become more proficient with data collection and presentation, be provided the time to collect necessary data, and receive needed training to acquire the skills to efficiently and effectively gather progress data to be used in the overall decision making process. In regards to ELLs, the data collected must reflect appropriate evidence-based instruction through the use of culturally responsive assessment techniques and devices. Effective data-driven decision making for ELLs can only occur if the data reflect culturally competent teaching and learning.

Problem-Solving Teams

Whether the team is called an intervention team, a problem-solving team, or by another name, it is important for a well-qualified, well-prepared team to examine screening, progress monitoring, and other data to determine the best course of action for a student who seems to be struggling. The team should include experts in language acquisition in all phases of instructional, referral, and assessment processes, particularly when students seem to be delayed in acquiring both their first language and English (Klingner et al., 2006). As noted previously, the team should consider contextual features, socio-cultural factors, school and program characteristics, and students' opportunities to learn in all phases of instructional, referral, and assessment processes.

Avoiding Assessment Pitfalls With ELLs

Throughout this book we have provided many examples and suggestions that relate to effective assessment of ELLs. In particular, when dealing with language development and usage, the concepts of dialect and register must be considered by practitioners in order to ensure nonbiased assessment. Assessment personnel must keep in mind a few key points:

1. Assessment conducted in English with ELLs becomes primarily an English test rather than a test of academic or social-emotional development.

2. Some form of dialect is used in any language spoken.

3. Diverse linguistic features (i.e., register) may create a situation where assessment does not accurately reflect the linguistic contexts within which the ELL has been instructed, and in turn this potentially yields invalid results.

Practitioners aware of these assessment concerns are more likely to use authentic assessment procedures and devices to form the basis for making effective decisions about ELLs in today's classrooms. In addition, Klingner and colleagues (2006) developed the following recommendations based on their review of research related to distinguishing between language acquisition and learning disabilities:

- Use alternative ways of assessing students' strengths to determine the upper limits of their potential.
- Conduct observations of students in different settings as part of any evaluation.
- Pay greater attention to cultural and affective considerations when evaluating students (e.g., sources of potential conflict, motivation).
- Give greater attention to students' native language and the role of language acquisition when determining whether a student may have learning disabilities.
- Consider that weak auditory processing skills could indicate language acquisition rather than a processing disorder or learning disabilities.
- Evaluate students in their first language as well as English to determine predictors of reading achievement.

PUTTING THE PIECES TOGETHER

The following guide may be used when considering the integrated implementation of the practical ideas above within the classroom. Table 7.1 provides a checklist to use to ensure the development and implementation of the best learning environment possible for ELLs, with one overall goal being to best understand language development needs as different from learning disability needs.

Table 7.1   Checklist of Components for Effective Learning Environments for ELLs

Instructions: Check each item addressed in the learning environment and share with problem-solving teams to best distinguish language difference from reading disability. Summary comments may also be documented at the end.

Optimal Learning Environment (Ruiz, 1995) . . .

___ Takes into account the student's sociocultural background and its effect on oral language, reading, writing, and second language learning

___ Takes into account the student's possible learning disabilities and its effect on oral language, reading, writing, and second language learning

___ Provides curriculum in a meaningful context where the communicative purpose is clear and authentic

___ Connects curriculum with student's personal experiences

___ Incorporates children's literature into reading, writing, and ESL lessons

___ Involves the parents as active partners in the instruction of their children

Explicit and Enhanced Literature Instruction (Gersten & Baker, 2000; Gersten, Brengelman, & Jiménez, 1994; Gersten & Jiménez, 1994) . . .

___ Provides frequent feedback on quality of performance and support

___ Provides adequate practice and activities that are interesting and engaging

___ Reinforces oral language with written cues and material

___ Pays attention to language: synonyms, idioms, etc.

___ Includes mediation and feedback: rephrasing and expanding responses

___ Promotes vocabulary development by modeling and explaining

Authentic Language Use (Escamilla, 1999) . . .

___ Uses best practices for ELLs that focus on language acquisition through authentic language use

___ Stresses the importance of ELLs being active participants in, rather than passive recipients of, language

___ Integrates the concept that authentic language use does not take place when language acquisition is treated as a separate subject in the student's day

Summary Comments:

As shown, a variety of educational practices assist practitioners to provide effective instruction to diverse learners. Educators can make certain that their classrooms support the use of these practices by periodically completing this guide.

In addition, Baca (2005) suggests that the following best practices should be an integral part of the education of ELLs:

- Prevention is viewed as a priority through professional collaboration.
- An ongoing, broadly-based, nonbiased assessment is provided.
- Early intervention is offered.
- Some of students' struggles are viewed as symptoms rather than disabilities.
- A gifted rather than a remedial approach is used.
- A broad range of special education services is offered in an inclusive environment.
- Instruction is provided in the student's primary language, with ESL in the content areas.
- General classroom teachers are involved in program planning and implementation.

Also, parents should be provided with maximum amounts of information in a language they understand, and should be meaningfully involved in planning and reinforcing instruction for their children.

CONCLUDING THOUGHTS ON FUTURE DIRECTIONS

As documented throughout this book, schools and school personnel in the 21st century have a critical need for interdisciplinary-trained special and general educators with specialized skills necessary to address linguistic and cultural diversity. These professionals can provide appropriate instructional programs and services to ELL students (Bos & Fletcher, 1997; Darling-Hammond, 2000; Dee, 2000). In a recent article, "Constructing 21st Century Teacher Education," Darling-Hammond (2006) stated that "schools of education must design programs that help prospective teachers to understand deeply a wide array of things about learning, social and cultural contexts, and teaching and be able to enact those understandings in complex classrooms serving increasingly diverse students" (p. 302). She suggests that the enterprise of teaching embark on a "mutual transformation agenda," in essence developing partnerships with schools and communities as a part of this agenda.

We urge that professional development emphasize cross-disciplinary and collaborative training that incorporates the multiple dimensions of teaching and learning discussed in this book. This suggests the use of collaborative teacher education models, which foster collaborative practices in which professionals are prepared to perform shared roles. The focus of classroom practice becomes more of a systems approach to meeting the needs of all children based on professional preparation using standards such as those developed by the Interstate New Teacher Assessment and Support Consortium standards (INTASC; 1992).

So, as we embark on the enterprise of teaching in the 21st century, we applaud legislative initiatives such as the RTI model. The model, when implemented early, systematically, precisely, and with fidelity using culturally responsive evidenced-based interventions, holds promise to increase the academic success of all students. Nevertheless, we would like to caution and reiterate that it is incumbent on us as professionals to weave sociocultural and psycho-cultural variables into the process to ensure that contextualization occurs at multiple levels (Tharp, 1989). As previously emphasized, the RTI model has the potential to become a more refined process with validated procedures to ensure academic success for all students. To this end, continued research and further validation of the RTI process for all students is necessary, especially for use with ELLs.

References

Abedi, J. (2004a, November). *Psychometric Issues in ELL Assessment and Special Education Eligibility.* Paper presented at the conference, English Language Learners Struggling to Learn: Emergent Research on Linguistic Differences and Learning Disabilities Conference, Tempe, AZ.

Abedi, J. (2004b). The No Child Left Behind Act and English language learners: Assessment and accountability issues. *Educational Researcher, 33* (1), 4–14.

Abedi, J., Lord, C., & Plummer, J. (1997). *Language background as a variable in NAEP mathematics performance* (CSE Tech. Rep. No. 429). Los Angeles: University of California, National Center for Research on Evaluation, Standards, and Student Testing.

Adams, M. J. (1990). *Beginning to read: Thinking and learning about print.* Cambridge, MA: MIT Press.

Adler, P. (1975). The transitional experiences: An alternative view of culture shock. *Journal of Humanistic Psychology, 15* (4), 13–23.

Algozzine, B., Christenson, S., & Ysseldyke, J. (1982). Probabilities associated with the referral to placement process. *Teacher Education and Special Education, 5,* 19–23.

Antunez, B. (2002). Implementing reading first with English language learners. *Directions in Language and Education, 15.* Retrieved May 9, 2006, from http://www.ncela.gwu.edu/pubs/directions/15.pdf

Applebee, A. (1989). *Center for the learning and teaching of literature.* Albany: State University of New York Education.

Artiles, A. J., Rueda, R., Salazar, J., & Higareda, I. (2005). Within-group diversity in minority disproportionate representation: English language learners in urban school districts. *Exceptional Children, 71,* 283–300.

Artiles, A. J., & Trent, S. C. (2000). Representation of culturally/linguistically diverse students. In C. R. Reynolds & E. Fletcher-Jantzen (Eds.), *Encyclopedia of special education, Vol. 1* (2nd ed., pp. 513–517). New York: Wiley.

August, D., & Hakuta, K. (1997). *Improving schooling for language minority children: A research agenda.* Washington, DC: National Research Council and Institute of Medicine, National Academy Press.

August, D., & Shanahan, T. (2006). *Developing literacy in second-language learners: Report of the National Literacy Panel on language-minority children and youth.* Mahwah, NJ: Lawrence Erlbaum Associates.

Baca, L., Baca, E., & de Valenzuela, J. S. (2004). Background and rationale for bilingual special education. In L. Baca & H. Cervantes (Eds.), *The bilingual special education interface* (4th ed., pp. 3–20). Upper Saddle River, NJ: Pearson, Merrill, Prentice Hall.

Baca, L., & Cervantes, H. (2004). *The bilingual special education interface*. Upper Saddle River, NJ: Pearson, Merrill, Prentice Hall.

Baca, L., & Clark, C. (1992). *EXITO: A dynamic team assessment approach for culturally diverse students*. Minneapolis, MN: Council for Exceptional Children.

Ball, E. W., & Blachman, B. A. (1988). Phoneme segmentation training: Effect on reading readiness. *Annals of Dyslexia, 38*, 208–225.

Barrera, M. (2004, November). *Roles of Definitional and Assessment Models in the Identification of New or Second Language Learners of English for Special Education*. Paper presented at the 2004 NCCRESt Conference, English Language Learners Struggling to Learn: Emergent Research on Linguistic Differences and Learning Disabilities. Tempe, AZ.

Barron, V., & Menken, K. (2002, August). What are the characteristics of the shortage of teachers qualified to teach English language learners? AskNCELA No. 14. Retrieved May 31, 2004, from http://www.ncela.gwu.edu/expert/faq/14 shortage.htm

Bateman, B. (1965). An educational view of a diagnostic approach to learning disorders. In J. Hellmuth (Ed.), *Learning Disorders: Vol. 1* (pp. 219–239). Seattle, WA: Special Child Publications.

Beck, I. L., McKeown, M. G., & Kucan, L. (2002). *Bringing words to life: Robust vocabulary instruction*. New York: Guilford Press.

Bernhard, J. K., Cummins, J., Campoy, F. I., & Ada, A. F. (2004, November). *Cognitive Engagement and Identity Investment in Literacy Development Among English Language Learners: Evidence From the Early Authors Program*. Paper presented at the 2004 NCCRESt Conference, English Language Learners Struggling to Learn: Emergent Research on Linguistic Differences and Learning Disabilities. Tempe, AZ.

Bernhard, J. K., Cummins, J., Campoy, F. I., Ada, A. F., Winsler, A., & Bleiker, C. (2006). Identity texts and literacy development among preschool English language learners: Enhancing learning opportunities for children at risk of learning disabilities. *Teachers College Record, 108* (11), 2380–2405.

Best, J. W., & Kahn, J. V. (1998). *Research in education* (8th ed.). Boston: Allyn & Bacon.

Bos, C., & Fletcher, T. (1997). Sociocultural considerations in learning disabilities research: Knowledge gaps and future directions. *Learning Disabilities Research and Practice, 12*, 92–99.

Brown-Chidsey, R., & Steege, M. W. (2005). *Response to intervention: Principles and strategies for effective practice*. New York: Guilford Press.

Buck, G. L., Polloway, E. A., Smith-Thomas, A., & Cook, K. W. (2003). Prereferral intervention processes: A survey of state practices. *Exceptional Children, 69* (3), 349–360.

Butler, F. A., & Stevens, R. (1997). Accommodation strategies for English language learners on large-scale assessments: Student characteristics and other considerations. CSE Technical Report 448. National Center for Research and Evaluation, Standards, and Student Testing. UCLA.

Camarota, S. (2001). *Immigrants and the schools*. Washington, DC: Urban Institute.

Canter, A. (2006). Problem solving and RTI: New roles for school psychologists. NASP *Communiqué, 34* (5). Available online from http://www.nasponline.org/publications/cq/cq345rti.aspx

Cazden, C. (2001). *Classroom discourse: The language of teaching and learning*. Portsmouth, NH: Heinemann.

Celce-Murcia, M., & Larsen-Freeman, D. (1983). *The grammar book: An ESL/EFL teacher's book.* Rowley, MA: Newbury House.

Chiappe, P., Siegel, L. A., & Gottardo, A. (2002). Reading-related skills of kindergartners from diverse linguistic backgrounds. *Applied Psycholinguistics, 23,* 95–116.

Chomsky, N. (1965). *Aspects of theory of syntax.* Cambridge, MA: MIT Press.

Christ, T. J., Burns, M. K., & Ysseldyke, J. E. (2005). Exploring RTI: Conceptual confusion within response-to-intervention vernacular: Clarifying meaningful differences. *NASP Communiqué, 34* (3). Available online from http://www.nasponline.org/publications/cq/cq343rti.aspx

Collier, C. (1988). *Assessing minority students with learning and behavior problems.* Boulder, CO: Hamilton Publications.

Collier, C. (2005). Separating language difference from disability. *NABE News, 28* (3), 13–17.

Collier, C., & Hoover, J. J. (1987a). *Cognitive learning styles for minority handicapped students.* Boulder, CO: Hamilton Publications.

Collier, C., & Hoover, J. J. (1987b). Sociocultural considerations when referring diverse children for learning disabilities. *LD Focus, 3* (1), 39–45.

Compton, D. L., Fuchs, D., Fuchs, L. S., & Bryant, J. D. (2006). Selecting at-risk readers in first grade for early intervention: A two-year longitudinal study of decision rules and procedures. *Journal of Educational Psychology, 98,* 394–409.

Crawford, J. (1999). *Bilingual education: History, politics, theory, and practice* (4th ed.). Los Angeles, CA: Bilingual Educational Services.

Crystal, D. (1997). *The Cambridge encyclopedia of language* (2nd ed.) Cambridge, England: Cambridge University Press.

Cummins, D. D., Kintsch, W., Reusser, K., & Weimer, R. (1988). The role of understanding in solving word problems. *Cognitive Psychology, 20,* 405–438.

Cummins, J. (1976). The influence of bilingualism on cognitive growth: A synthesis of research findings and explanatory hypotheses. *Working Papers on Bilingualism, 9,* 1–43.

Cummins, J. (1979). Linguistic interdependence and the educational development of bilingual children. *Review of Educational Research, 49,* 221–51.

Cummins, J. (1981). The role of primary language development in promoting educational success for language minority students. In California State Department of Education (Ed.), *Schooling and language minority students: A theoretical framework* (pp. 3–50). Sacramento: California State Department of Education.

Cummins, J. (1986). Empowering minority students: A framework for intervention. *Harvard Educational Review, 56,* 18–36.

Cummins, J. (1989). A theoretical framework for bilingual special education. *Exceptional Children, 56* (3), 111–19.

Cummins, J. (2000). *Language, power and pedagogy: Bilingual children in the crossfire.* Clevedon, England: Multilingual Matters.

Curtiss, S., MacSwan, J., Schaeffer, J., & Sano, T. (2004). GCS: A grammatical coding system for natural language data. *Behavior Research Methods, Instruments, and Computers, 34* (3), 459–480.

Darling-Hammond, L. (2000). Teacher quality and student achievement: A review of state policy evidence. *Education Policy Analysis Archives, 8,* 1–67.

Darling-Hammond, L. (2006). Constructing 21st-century teacher education. *Journal of Teacher Education, 57,* 300–314.

De Avila, E. A., & Duncan, S. E. (1990). *LAS: Language assessment scales oral: Scoring and interpretation manual, Spanish, level 2B.* Monterey, CA: CTB/McGraw-Hill.

De Avila, E. A., & Duncan, S. E. (1994). LAS: *Language assessment scales oral: Administration manual, Español, form 1b.* Monterey, CA: CTB/McGraw-Hill.

Dee, T. S. (2000). *Teachers, race and student achievement in a randomized experiment.* Unpublished manuscript, Swarthmore College, Pennsylvania.

Delpit, L. (1995). *Other people's children* (1st ed.). New York: The New Press.

Deno, S. L. (2005). Problem-solving assessment. In R. Brown-Chidsey (Ed.), *Assessment for intervention: A problem-solving approach* (pp. 10–40). New York: Guilford.

Donovan, M. S., & Cross, C. (Eds.) (2002). *Minority students in special and gifted education.* Washington, DC: National Academy Press.

Doris, J. L. (1993). Defining a learning disability: A history of the search for consensus. In G. R. Lyon, D. B. Gray, J. F. Kavanagh, & N. A. Krasnegor (Eds.), *Better understanding learning disabilities* (pp. 97–116). Baltimore: Paul Brookes Publishing.

Duncan, S. E., & De Avila, E. A. (1986a). *Pre-LAS Espanol* (2nd ed.). Monterey, CA: CTB/McGraw-Hill.

Duncan, S. E., & De Avila, E. A. (1986b). *Scoring and interpretation manual for the Pre-LAS Espanol* (2nd ed.). Monterey, CA: CTB/McGraw-Hill.

Durgunoglu, A. Y., Nagy, W. E., & Hancin-Bhatt, B. J. (1993). Cross-language transfer of phonological awareness. *Journal of Educational Psychology, 85,* 453–465.

Durkin, D. (1978-1979). What classroom observations reveal about reading comprehension instruction. *Reading Research Quarterly, 14* (4), 481–533.

Escamilla, K. (1993). Promoting biliteracy: Issues in promoting English literacy in students acquiring literacy. In J. Tinajero & A. Flor Ada (Eds.), *The power of two languages*: *Literacy and biliteracy for Spanish speaking children* (pp. 220–233.). New York: MacMillan/McGraw-Hill.

Escamilla, K. (1999). *Second language acquisition.* On Educating Culturally and Linguistically Diverse Students: A Professional Development Resource Series.

Escamilla, K., Baca, L., Hoover, J., & Almanza de Schonewise, E. (2005). *An analysis of limited English proficient student achievement on Colorado state reading, writing and math performance standards.* Final Technical Report Submitted for Field Initiated Research Project T292B010005. US Department of Education.

Escamilla, K., Chavez, L., Fitts, S., Mahon, E., & Vigil, P. (2003). *Limited English proficient students and the Colorado students assessment program (CSAP): The state of the state, 2002–2003.* Denver: Colorado Association for Bilingual Education.

Escamilla, K., Chavez, L. & Vigil, P. (2005, March/April). Rethinking the gap: High stakes testing and Spanish-speaking students in Colorado. *Journal of Teacher Education, 56* (2), 132–144.

Escamilla, K., & Escamilla, M. (2003). *Literature review: Best practices for Latino preschool children.* ALMAR Research Report. Boulder County Head Start, City of Boulder Children, Youth and Families Division: Boulder, CO.

Fairbanks, S., Sugai, G., Guardino, D., & Lathrop, M. (2007). Response to intervention: Examining classroom behavior support in second grade. *Exceptional Children, 73,* 288–310.

Farr, M., & Ball, A. F. (1999). Standard English. In B. Spolsky (Ed.), *Concise encyclopedia of educational linguistics* (pp. 205–208). Oxford, UK: Elsevier.

Ferris, D. R. (2002). *Treatment of error in second language student writing.* Ann Arbor, MI: The University of Michigan Press.

Figueroa, R. (1989). Psychological testing of linguistic-minority students: Knowledge gaps and regulations. *Exceptional Children, 56*, 145–153.

Figueroa, R. (2002). Toward a new model of assessment. In A. J. Artiles & A. A. Ortiz (Eds.), *English language learners with special education needs: Identification, assessment and instruction* (pp. 51–63). Washington, DC: Center for Applied Linguistics.

Figueroa, R. A., & Newsome, P. (2004, November). *The Diagnosis of Learning Disabilities in English Language Learners: Is It Nondiscriminatory?* Paper presented at the 2004 NCCRESt Conference, English Language Learners Struggling to Learn: Emergent Research on Linguistic Differences and Learning Disabilities. Tempe, AZ.

Foster, M. (1993). "Savage inequalities": Where have we come from? Where are we going? *Educational Theory, 43* (1), 23–32.

Francis, D. J., Rivera, M., Lesaux, N., Kieffer, M., & Rivera, H. (2006). *Research-based recommendations for instruction and academic interventions: Practical guidelines for the education of English language learners.* Houston, TX: Center on Instruction.

Freeman, G. G. (1978, June). *Interdisciplinary Evaluation of Children's Primary Language Skills.* Paper presented at the World Congress on Future Special Education, First, Stirling, Scotland. (ERIC Document Reproduction Service No. ED157341)

Fuchs, D., Mock, D., Morgan, P. L., & Young, C. (2003). Responsiveness-to-instruction intervention: Definitions, evidence, and implications for the learning disabilities construct. *Learning Disabilities: Research & Practice, 18* (3), 157–171.

Fuchs, L. S., Fuchs, D., & Hollenbeck, K. N. (2007). Extending responsiveness to intervention to mathematics at first and third grades. *Learning Disabilities Research & Practice, 22*, 13–24.

Gallego, M. A., Duran, G. Z., & Reyes, E. I. (2004, November). *It Depends . . . : A Socio-historical Account of the Definition and Methods of Identification of Learning Disabilities.* Paper presented at the National Center for Culturally Responsive Educational Systems Research Conference on English Language Learners Struggling to Learn: Emergent Research on Linguistic Differences and Learning Disabilities, Scottsdale, AZ.

Garcia, E. (2001). *Hispanic education in the United States: Raices y alas.* Lanham, ML: Rowman and Littfield Publishers Inc.

Garcia, E. (2004, November). *Who are these linguistically and culturally diverse students?* Paper presented at the National Center for Culturally Responsive Educational Systems Research Conference on English Language Learners Struggling to Learn: Emergent Research on Linguistic Differences and Learning Disabilities, Scottsdale, AZ.

Garcia, G. (2000). *Lessons from research: What is the length of time it takes limited English proficient students to acquire English and succeed in an all English classroom?* Washington, DC: National Clearinghouse for Bilingual Education.

Genesee, F. (Ed.). (1994). Introduction. In F. Genesee (Ed.), *Educating second language children: The whole child, the whole curriculum, the whole community* (pp. 1–11). Cambridge, UK: Cambridge University Presson Linguistic Differences and Learning.

Genesee, F., & Nicoladis, E. (2006). Bilingual first language acquisition. In E. Hoff & M. Shatz (Eds.), *Handbook of language development* (pp. 324–342). Oxford, England: Blackwell.

Gentile, L. (2004). *The oracy instructional guide.* Carlsbad, CA: Dominie Press.

Gersten, R., & Baker, S. (2000). What we know about effective instructional practices for English-language learners. *Exceptional Children, 66,* 454–470.

Gersten, R., Brengelman, S., & Jimenez, R. (1994). Effective instruction for culturally and linguistically diverse students: A reconceptualization. *Focus on Exceptional Children, 27* (1), 1–16.

Gersten, R., & Dimino, J. A. (2006). New directions in research: RTI (Response to Intervention): Rethinking special education for students with reading difficulties (yet again). *Reading Research Quarterly, 41,* 99–108.

Gersten, R., & Jimenez, R. (1994). A delicate balance: Enhancing literacy instruction for students of English as a second language. *Reading Teacher, 47,* 438–449.

Gleitman, L., & Landau, B. (1994). *The acquisition of the lexicon.* Cambridge, MA: MIT Press.

Goldenberg, C. (2006). *Improving achievement for English learners: Conclusions from 2 research reviews.* Available online from http://www.colorincolorado.org/article/12918

Goldenberg, C., & Gallimore, R. (1991). Local knowledge, research knowledge and educational change: A case study of early Spanish reading improvement. *Educational Researcher, 20* (8), 2–14.

Good, R. H., & Kaminski, R. A. (Eds.). (2002). *Dynamic Indicators of Basic Early Literacy Skills* (6th ed.). Eugene, OR: Institute for the Development of Educational Achievement.

Good, R. H., Simmons, D. C., & Smith, S. B. (1998). Effective academic interventions in the United States: Evaluating and enhancing the acquisition of early reading skills. *Educational and Child Psychology, 15,* 56–70.

Gordon, P. (1996). The truth-value judgment task. In D. McDaniel, C. McKee, & H. S. Cairns (Eds.), *Methods for assessing children's syntax* (211–232). Cambridge: MIT Press.

Gottlieb, J., Alter, M., Gottlieb, B. W., & Wishner, J. (1994). Special education in urban America: It's not justifiable for many. *The Journal of Special Education, 27,* 453–465.

Gottlieb, J., Alter, M., Gottlieb, B. W., Wishner, J., & Yoshida, R. K. (1990). *Final report for year III of the consulting teacher program.* Report submitted to New York State Education Department, Office for Children with Handicapping Conditions.

Greene, J. (1997). A meta-analysis of the Rossell and Baker review of bilingual education research. *Bilingual Research Journal, 21,* 103–122.

Grossman, H. (1995). *Special education in a diverse society.* Boston: Allyn & Bacon.

Haager, D. (2004, November). *Promoting Reading Achievement for English Language Learners Learning in English: A Case for Explicit Instruction.* Paper presented at the 2004 NCCRESt Conference, English Language Learners Struggling to Learn: Emergent Research on Linguistic Differences and Learning Disabilities, Tempe, AZ.

Haliday, M. A. K. (1978). *Language as social semiotic: The social interpretation of language and meaning.* London, UK: Edward Arnold Publishers.

Hallahan, D. P., & Mercer, C. (2002). Learning disabilities: Historical perspectives. In R. Bradley, L. Danielson, & D. P. Hallahan (Eds.), *Identification of learning disabilities: Research to practice* (pp. 1–68). Mahwah, NJ: Lawrence Erlbaum Associates.

Hallahan, D. P., & Mock, D. R. (2003). A brief history of the field of learning disabilities. In H. L. Swanson, K. R. Harris, & S. Graham (Eds.), *Handbook of learning disabilities* (pp. 16–29). New York: Guilford Press.

Hammill, D. D. (1990). On defining learning disabilities: An emerging consensus. *Journal of Learning Disabilities, 23*, 74–84.

Harper, C. A., & de Jong, E. J. (2004). Misconceptions about teaching ELLs. *Journal of Adolescent and Adult Literacy, 48* (2), 152–162.

Harry, B., & Klingner, J. (2005). *Why are so many minority students in special education? Understanding race and disability in schools.* New York: Teachers College Press.

Hiebert, E. H., Pearson, P. D., Taylor, B. M., Richardson, V., & Paris, S. G. (1998). *Every child a reader: Applying reading research to the classroom.* Center for the Improvement of Earl Reading Achievement. Ann Arbor, MI: University of Michigan School of Education.

Hodgkinson, H. (2005, November 30). *Who are the rising stars? The demographics of language in a pluralistic nation and shrinking world.* Rising Star Summit IV: Celebrate our Rising Stars. Washington, DC.

Hofstetter, C. H. (2003). Contextual and mathematics accommodation test effects for English language learners. *Applied Measurement in Education, 16* (2), 159–188.

Hoover, J. J. (2001). *Assessment of English language learners.* CD-ROM training module. Boulder, CO: BUENO Center, University of Colorado, Boulder.

Hoover, J. J. (2005). Special challenges for special needs. In J. J. Hoover (Ed.), *Current issues in special education: Meeting diverse needs in the twenty-first century.* Boulder, CO: BUENO Center, University of Colorado.

Hoover, J. J. (2006, April). *Framework for Culturally Competent Response to Intervention.* Invited presentation delivered at the New York City Public Schools, Summit on Differentiated Instruction and Academic Interventions, New York, NY.

Hoover, J. J., Baca, L. M., Love, E., & Seanz, L. P. (in review). State of the states in implementing response to intervention. *Intervention in School and Clinic.*

Hoover, J. J., & Collier, C. (1985). Referring culturally different children: Sociocultural considerations. *Academic Therapy, 20* (4), 503–509.

Hoover, J. J., & Collier, C. (2003). *Learning Styles* (CD-ROM). Boulder, CO: University of Colorado, BUENO Center, School of Education.

Hoover, J. J., Klingner, J. K., Baca, L. M., & Patton, J. M. (2008). *Teaching culturally and linguistically diverse exceptional learners.* Columbus, OH: Merrill.

Hunt, K. W. (1965). *Grammatical structures written at three grade levels* (Research Rep. No. 3). Urbana, IL: National Council of Teachers of English.

Individuals with Disabilities Education Act Amendments of 1997, Pub. L. No. 105-17, SS 601 *et seq.,* 111 Stat. 37 (1997).

Individuals with Disabilities Education Improvement Act (IDEA, 2004) H.R. 1350. Retrieved March 14, 2007, from http://thomas.loc.gov/cgi-bin/query/z?c108:h.1350.enr:

Interstate New Teacher Assessment and Support Consortium. (1992). *Model standards for beginning teacher licensing, assessment and development: A resource for state dialogue.* Council of Chief State School Officers. Washington, DC. Available online from http://www.ccsso.org/content/pdfs/corestrd.pdf#search=%22INTASC%22

IRIS Center for Training Enhancements. (no date). *Star Legacy Module-RtI.* Retrieved October, 2007, from http://iris.peabody.vanderbilt.edu/resources .html

Jacobson, R., & Faltis, C. (Eds.). (1990). *Language distribution issues in bilingual schooling.* Clevedon, England: Multicultural Matters.

Jiménez, R. T. (1997). The strategic reading abilities and potential of five low-literacy Latina/o readers in middle school. *Reading Research Quarterly, 32* (3), 224–243.

Juel, C. (1988). Learning to read and write: A longitudinal study of 54 children from first through fourth grades. *Journal of Educational Psychology, 80,* 437–47.

Kendler, A. C. (2002). *Survey of the States Limited English Proficient Students 2000–2001.* Washington, DC: Office of English Acquisition, Language Enhancement and Academic Achievement for Limited English Proficient Students. U.S. Department of Education.

Kirk, S. A. (1962). *Educating exceptional children.* Boston: Houghton Mifflin.

Klingner, J. K., Artiles, A. J., Kozleski, E., Harry, B., Zion, S., Tate, W., Durán, G. Z., & Riley, D. (2005). Addressing the disproportionate representation of culturally and linguistically diverse students in special education through culturally responsive educational systems. *Education Policy Analysis Archives, 13*(38), 1–39. Available online from http://epaa.asu.edu/epaa/v13n38/

Klingner, J. K., Artiles, A., & Mendez-Barletta, L. (2004, November). *English Language Learners and Learning Disabilities: A Critical Review of the Literature.* Paper presented at the National Center for Culturally Responsive Educational Systems Research Conference on English Language Learners Struggling to Learn: Emergent Research on Linguistic Differences and Learning Disabilities, Scottsdale, AZ.

Klingner, J. K., & Edwards, P. (2006). Cultural considerations with response to intervention models. *Reading Research Quarterly, 41,* 108–117.

Klingner, J. K., & Harry, B. (2004). The special education referral and decision-making process for English language learners-Child study team meetings and staffings. Paper presented at the 2004 NCCRESt Conference, English Language Learners Struggling to Learn: Emergent Research on Linguistic Differences and Learning Disabilities, Tempe, AZ.

Klingner, J. K., Urbach, J., Golos, D., et al. (2007, July). *How Do Special Education Teachers Promote the Reading Comprehension of Students with LD?* Paper presented at the International Academy for Research on Learning Disabilities Annual Meeting, Lake Bled, Slovenia.

Krashen, S. D. (1981). *Principles and practice in second language acquisition. English language teaching series.* London: Prentice-Hall International.

Lachat, M. A. (2004). *Standards-based instruction and assessment for English language learners.* Thousand Oaks, CA: Corwin Press.

Ladson-Billings, G. (2005). But that's just good practice! The case for culturally relevant pedagogy. *Theory into Practice, 34* (3), 159–165.

Langdon, H. W. (1989). Language disorder or language difference? Assessing the language skills of Hispanic students. *Exceptional Children, 56,* 160–167.

Lanza, E. (1992). Can bilingual two-year-olds code-switch? *Journal of Child Language, 19,* 633–658.

Lee, J. (2002). Racial and ethnic achievement gap trends: Reversing the progress towards equity. *Educational Researcher, 32,* 3–12.

Linan-Thompson, S., Vaughn, S., Prater, K., & Cirino, P. T. (2004). *The Response to Intervention of English Language Learners At-Risk for Reading Problems.* Paper presented at the 2004 NCCRESt Conference, English Language Learners Struggling to Learn: Emergent Research on Linguistic Differences and Learning Disabilities, Tempe, AZ.

Lindsey, K. A., Manis, F. R., & Bailey, C. E. (2003). Prediction of first-grade reading in Spanish-speaking English-language learners. *Journal of Educational Psychology, 95,* 482-494.

Loe, S. A., & Miranda, A. H. (2002). Assessment of culturally and linguistically diverse learners with behavioral disorders. In G. Cartledge, K. Y. Tam, S. A. Loe, A. H. Miranda, M. C., Lamberts, C. D. Kea, & S.E. Simmons-Reed (Eds.), *Culturally and linguistically diverse students with behavioral disorders* (pp.25–36). Arlington, VA: Council for Exceptional Children (Council for Children with Behavioral Disorders Division).

MacSwan, J. (1999). *A minimalist approach to intrasentential code switching.* New York: Garland Press.

MacSwan, J. (2000). The threshold hypothesis, semilingualism, and other contributions to a deficit view of linguistic minorities. *Hispanic Journal of Behavioral Sciences, 22* (1), 3–45.

MacSwan, J. (2004, November). *The "Non-Non" Crisis: How Language Assessments Mislead Us About the Native Language Ability of English Learners.* Paper presented at the 2004 NCCRESt Conference, English Language Learners Struggling to Learn: Emergent Research on Linguistic Differences and Learning Disabilities, Tempe, AZ.

MacSwan, J., & Rolstad, K. (2003). Linguistic diversity, schooling and social class: Rethinking our conception of language proficiency in language minority education. In C.B. Paulston & R. Tucker (Eds.), *Essential readings in sociolinguistics* (pp. 329–340). Oxford: Blackwell.

MacSwan, J., Rolstad, K., & Glass, G. (2002). Do some school-age children have no language? Some problems of construct validity in the Pre-LAS Espanol. *Bilingual Research Journal, 26* (2), 395–420.

Mayer, M. (1969). *Frog where are you?* New York: Dial Books for Young Readers, Inc.

McCardle, P., Mele-McCarthy, J., & Leos, K. (2005). English language learners and learning disabilities: Research agenda and implications for practice. *Learning Disabilities Research & Practice, 20* (1), 68.

McLaughlin, B. (1984). *Second language acquisition in childhood: Vol. 1. Preschool children* (2nd ed.). Hillsdale, NJ: Lawrence Erlbaum Associates.

McLaughlin, B. (1992). *Myths and misconceptions about second language learning: What every teacher needs to unlearn.* Santa Cruz, CA: National Center for Research in Cultural Diversity and Second Language Learning.

Menken, K., & Antunez, B. (2001). An overview of the preparation and certification of teachers working with limited English proficient (LEP) Students. Washington, DC: National Clearinghouse for Bilingual Education and ERIC Clearinghouse on Teaching and Teacher Education. Available online from http://www.eric.ed.gov/ERICDocs/data/ericdocs2sql/content_storage_ 01/0000019b/80/29/cb/0e.pdf

Merino, B., & Quintanar, R. (1989). The recruitment of minority students into teaching careers: A Status report of effective approaches. Boulder, CO: Far West Regional Holmes Group, University of Colorado.

Messick, S. (1989). Validity. In R. L. Linn (Ed), *Educational measurement* (3rd ed., pp. 13–103). Washington, DC: American Council on Education and National Council on Measurement in Education.

Mestre, J. P. (1988). The role of language comprehension in mathematics and problem solving. In R. R. Cocking & J. P. Mestre (Eds.), *Linguistic and cultural influences on learning mathematics* (pp. 200–220). Hillsdale, NJ: Lawrence Erlbaum Associates.

Moll, L. C., & Greenberg, J. B. (1990). Creating zones of possibilities: Combining social contexts for instruction. In L. C. Moll (Ed.), *Vygotsky and education: Instructional implications and applications of sociohistorical psychology* (pp. 319–348). New York: Cambridge University Press.

Moore, K. J., Fifield, M. B., Spira, D. A., & Scarlato, M. (1998). Child study team decision making in special education: Improving the process. *Remedial and Special Education, 10,* 50–58.

National Association of State Directors of Special Education (NASDSE). (2005). *Response to intervention: Policy considerations and implementation.* Available online from NASDSE Publications http://www.nasdse.org

National Center for Educational Statistics (2000). Annual report, 2000. Washington, DC: US Department of Education.

National Center for Educational Statistics. (2004). *Overview of public elementary and secondary schools and districts: School year 2001–2002.* Washington, DC: U.S. Department of Education.

National Reading Panel. (2000). *Teaching children to read: An evidence-based assessment of the scientific research literature on reading and its implications for reading instruction: summary report.* Washington, DC: National Institute of Child Health and Development.

Nazarro, J. N. (Ed.) (1981). *Culturally diverse exceptional children.* Arlington, VA: Council for Exceptional Children.

NCCRESt Position Statement (2005). *Cultural considerations and challenges in response to intervention models* (Author). NCCRESt

No Child Left Behind Act (2001). Public Law 107–110, 115 Stat. 1425.

Orosco, M. (2007). *Response to intervention with Latino English language learners: A school-based study.* Unpublished doctoral dissertation, University of Colorado at Boulder.

Orr, E. W. (1987). *Twice as less: Black English and the performance of black students in mathematics and science.* New York: W. W. Norton.

Ortiz, A. A. (1997). LD occurring concomitantly with linguistic differences. *Journal of LD, 30,* 321–332.

Ortiz, A. A. (2002). Prevention and early intervention. In A. J. Artiles & A. A. Ortiz (Eds.), *English language learners with special needs* (pp. 31–48). Washington, DC: Center for Applied Linguistics and Delta Systems.

Ortiz, A. A., & Maldonado-Colon, E. (1986). Recognizing learning disabilities in bilingual children: How to lessen inappropriate referrals of language minority students to special education. *Journal of Reading, Writing and Learning Disabilities International, 2* (1), 43–56.

Ovando, O., Collier, V., & Combs, M. (2003). Bilingual and ESL classrooms: Teaching in multicultural contexts. Boston: McGraw Hill.

Peregoy, S. F., & Boyle, O. F. (2001). *Reading, writing, and learning in ESL: A resource book for K–12 teachers* (3rd Ed.) New York: Addison Wesley Longman.

Pinker, S. (1994). *The language instinct: How the mind creates languages.* New York: William Morrow and Company.

Portes, A., & Rumbaut, R. G. (2001). *Legacies: The story of the immigrant second generation.* Berkeley, CA: University of California Press.

Preston, D. R. (2003). *American dialect research.* Philadelphia, PA: John Benjamins.

Reilly, J. S., Marchman, V., & Bates, E. A. (1998). Narratives in children with early focal brain damage. *Brain and Language, 61* (3), 335–337.

Reyes, M. d. l. L. (1991). A process approach to literacy instruction for Spanish-speaking students: In search of a best fit. In I. E. H. Heibert (Ed.), *Literacy for a diverse society: Perspectives, practices and policies* (pp. 157–171). New York: Teachers College Press.

Reyes, M. d. l. L., & McCollum, P. (1992). *Diversity and literacy in schools: Issues for urban society.* New York: Teachers College Press.

Rolstad, K., Mahoney, K., & Glass, G. (2005). The big picture: A meta-analysis of program effectiveness research on English language learners. *Educational Policy, 19,* 572–594.

Rueda, R., MacGillivray, L., & Monzó, L. (2001). *Engaged reading: A multilevel approach to considering sociocultural factors with diverse learners.* Ann Arbor, MI: Center for the Improvement of Early Reading Achievement.

Rueda, R., & Windmueller, M. (2004, November). *English Language Learners, Learning Disabilities, and Overrepresentation: A Multiple Level Analysis.* Paper presented at the National Center for Culturally Responsive Educational Systems Research Conference on English Language Learners Struggling to Learn: Emergent Research on Linguistic Differences and Learning Disabilities, Scottsdale, AZ.

Ruiz, N. (1988). *The nature of bilingualism: Implications for special education.* Sacramento: California State Department of Education, Resources in Special Education.

Ruiz, N. (1989). An optimal learning environment for Rosemary. *Exceptional Children, 56,* 29–41.

Ruiz, R. (1988). Orientations in language planning. In S. McKay & S. Wong (Eds.), *Language diversity: Problem or resource?* (pp. 3 25). Cambridge, MA: Newbury House Publishers.

Rumbaut, R. (1997). Ties that bind: Immigration and immigrant families in the United States. In A. Booth, C. Crouter, & N. Landale (Eds.), *Immigration and the family: Research and policy on U.S. immigrants* (pp. 3–45). Hillsdale, NJ: Lawrence Erlbaum Associates.

Rutter, M., & Yule, W. (1975). The concept of specific reading retardation. *Journal of Child Psychiatry, 16* (3), 181–197.

Scanlon, D. M., & Vellutino, F. R. (1996). Prerequisite skills, early instruction, and success in first grade reading: Selected results from a longitudinal study. *Mental Retardation and Development Disabilities, 2,* 54–63.

Selinker, L. (1972). Interlanguage. *International Review of Applied Linguistics, 10,* 201–231.

Selinker, L., Swain, M., & Dumas, G. (1975). The interlanguage hypothesis extended to children. *Language Learning, 25* (1), 139–152.

Slavin, R. E., & Cheung, A. (2005). A synthesis of research on language of reading instruction for English language learners. *Review of Educational Research, 75,* 247–284.

Slobin, D. I. (1968). Recall of full and truncated passive sentences in connected discourse. *Journal of Verbal Learning and Verbal Behavior, 7,* 876–881.

Snow, C. (2002). Reading for understanding: Toward an R&D program in reading comprehension. Santa Monica, CA: RAND.

Snow, C. S., Burns, S. M., & Griffin, P. (1998). *Preventing reading difficulties in young children.* Washington, DC: National Academy Press.

Solano-Flores, G. (2004, November). *Language, Dialect, and Register: Sociolinguistics and the Estimation of Measurement Error in the Testing of English-Language Learners.* Paper presented at the Conference, English Language Learners Struggling to Learn: Emergent Research on Linguistic Differences and Learning Disabilities Conference, Tempe, AZ.

Solano-Flores, G., & Trumbull, E. (2003). Examining language in context: The need for new research and practice paradigms in the testing of English language learners. *Education Researcher, 32* (2), 3–13.

Spanos, G., Rhodes, N. C., Dale, T. C., & Crandall, J. (1988). Linguistic features of mathematical problem solving: Insights and applications. In R. R. Cocking & J. P. Mestre (Eds.), *Linguistic and cultural influences on learning mathematics* (pp. 221–240). Hillsdale, NJ: Lawrence Erlbaum Associates.

Special Issues Analysis Center. (1995). *Digest of educational statistics for limited English proficient students.* Washington, DC: U.S. Department of Education, Office of Bilingual Education and Minority Languages Affairs.

Stanovich, K. E. (1986). Matthew effects in reading: Some consequences of individual differences in the acquisition of literacy. *Reading Research Quarterly, 21* (4), 360–407.

Stefanakis, E. H. (1998). *Whose judgment counts: Assessing bilingual children K–3.* Portsmouth, NH: Heinemann.

Stuebing, K. K., Fletcher, J. M., LeDoux, J. M., Lyon, G. R., Shaywitz, S. E., & Shaywitz, B. A. (2002). Validity of IQ-discrepancy classifications of reading disabilities: A meta-analysis. *American Educational Research Journal, 39*, 469–518.

Swain, M. (1995). Three functions of output in second language learning. In G. Cook & B. Seidlhofer (Eds.), *Principles and practice in the study of language.* Oxford: Oxford University Press.

Tager-Flusberg, H. (1997). Putting words together: Morphology and syntax in the preschool years. In J. Berko-Gleason (Ed.), *The development of language* (pp. 159–209). Boston: Allyn and Bacon.

Tharp, R. G. (1989). Psycho-cultural variables and constants: Effects on teaching and learning in schools. *American Psychologist, 44*, 349–359.

Tharp, R. G. (1997). *From at-risk to excellence: Research, theory, and principles for practice* (Research Report 1). Santa Cruz, CA: Center for Research on Education, Diversity and Excellence.

Thomas, W., & Collier, V. (1997). *School effectiveness for language minority students.* Alexandria, VA: National Clearinghouse for Bilingual Education.

Thomas, W., & Collier, V. (2002). *A national study of school effectiveness for language minority students' long-term achievement.* Center for Research on Education, Diversity & Excellence. Available online from http://www.crede.ucsc.edu/research/llaa/1.1es.html

Timm, L. A. (1993). Bilingual code-switching: An overview of research. In B. J. Merino, H. T. Trueba, & F. A. Samaniego (Eds.), *Language and culture in learning: Teaching Spanish to native speakers of Spanish* (pp. 94–112). Bristol, PA: Falmer Press.

University of Texas Center for Reading and Language Arts. (2003). *3-tier reading model: Reducing reading difficulties for kindergarten through third grade students.* Austin: UT System/Texas Education Agency.

U.S. Department of Education. (2003). National Assessment of Educational Progress. Washington, DC: U.S. Department of Education. Available online from http://nces.ed.gov/nationsreportcard/reading/results2003/natachieve-re-g4.asp

U.S. Office of Education. (1968). *The first annual report of National Advisory Committee on Handicapped Children.* Washington, DC: U.S. Department of Health, Education and Welfare.

Valadez, C., MacSwan, J., & Martinez, C. (1997, April). *Toward a New View of Low Achieving Bilinguals: Syntactic Competence in Designated "Semilinguals."* Paper presented at the annual meeting of the American Educational Research Association, Chicago.

Valdés, G. (1980). Is code-switching interference, integration, or neither? In E. L. Blansitt, Jr. & R. V. Teschner (Eds.), *A Festschrift for Jacob Ornstein: Studies in general linguistics and sociolinguistics* (pp. 314–25). New York: Newbury House.

Valdés, G. (2001). *Learning and not learning English: Latino students in American schools.* New York: Teacher College Press.

Valdés, G., & Figueroa, R. (1994). *Bilingualism and testing: A special case of bias.* Norwood, New Jersey: Ablex Publishing.

Vaughn, S., & Fuchs, L. S. (2003). Redefining learning disabilities as inadequate response to treatment: the promise and potential problems. *Learning Disabilities Research and Practice, 18* (3), 137–146.

Wardhaugh, R. (2002). *An introduction to sociolinguistics* (4th ed.). Oxford, UK: Blackwell

Wexler, K., & Culicover, P. W. (1980). *Formal principles of language acquisition.* Cambridge, MA: MIT Press.

Wilkinson, C. Y., Ortiz, A., & Robertson-Courtney, P. (2004, November). *Appropriate Eligibility Determination for English Language Learners Suspected of Having Reading-Related Learning Disabilities: Linking School History, Prereferral, Referral and Assessment Data.* Paper presented at the 2004 NCCRESt Conference, English Language Learners Struggling to Learn: Emergent Research on Linguistic Differences and Learning Disabilities, Tempe, AZ.

Willig, A. (1985). A meta-analysis of selected studies on the effectiveness of bilingual education. *Review of Educational Research, 55,* 269–317.

Wolfe, P., & Brandt, R. (1998). What do we know from brain research? *Educational Leadership, 56* (3), 8–13.

Wolfram, W. (2000). On construction vernacular dialect norms. In J. P. Boyle & A. Okrent (Eds.), *CLS 36: The 36th meeting of the Chicago Linguistic Society, 2000.* Chicago: Chicago Linguistic Society.

Wong Fillmore, L. (2000). Loss of family languages: Should educators be concerned? *Theory into Practice, 39* (4), 203–210.

Woodcock, R., & Munoz-Sandoval, A. (1993). *Woodcock-Munoz language survey. Spanish Form.* Itasca, IL: Riverside Publishing.

Ysseldyke, J. (2005). Assessment and decision making for students with learning disabilities: What if this is as good as it gets? *Learning Disability Quarterly, 28,* 125–128.

Zehler, A., Hopstock, P., Fleishman, H., & Greniuk, C. (1994). *An examination of assessment of limited English proficient students.* Arlington, VA: Special Issues Analysis Center.

Index

CORWIN PRESS

The Corwin Press logo—a raven striding across an open book—represents the union of courage and learning. Corwin Press is committed to improving education for all learners by publishing books and other professional development resources for those serving the field of PreK–12 education. By providing practical, hands-on materials, Corwin Press continues to carry out the promise of its motto: **"Helping Educators Do Their Work Better."**